D0553982

3 0600 00415 1057

THE SCARECROW AUTHOR BIBLIOGRAPHIES

1. John Steinbeck (Tetsumaro Hayashi). 1973.
   See also no. 64.
2. Joseph Conrad (Theodore G. Ehrsam). 1969.
3. Arthur Miller (Tetsumaro Hayashi). 2d ed. 1976.
4. Katherine Anne Porter (Waldrip & Bauer). 1969.
5. Philip Freneau (Philip M. Marsh). 1970.
6. Robert Greene (Tetsumaro Hayashi). 1971.
7. Benjamin Disraeli (R.W. Stewart). 1972.
8. John Berryman (Richard W. Kelly). 1972.
9. William Dean Howells (Vito J. Brenni). 1973.
10. Jean Anouilh (Kathleen W. Kelly). 1973.
11. E.M. Forster (Alfred Borrello). 1973.
12. The Marquis de Sade (E. Pierre Chanover). 1973.
13. Alain Robbe-Grillet (Dale W. Frazier). 1973.
14. Northrop Frye (Robert D. Denham). 1974.
15. Federico Garcia Lorca (Laurenti & Siracusa). 1974.
16. Ben Jonson (Brock & Welsh). 1974.
17. Four French Dramatists: Eugène Brieux, François de Curel, Emile Fabre, Paul Hervieu (Edmund F. Santa Vicca). 1974.
18. Ralph Waldo Ellison (Jacqueline Covo). 1974.
19. Philip Roth (Bernard F. Rodgers, Jr.). 1974.
20. Norman Mailer (Laura Adams). 1974.
21. Sir John Betjeman (Margaret Stapleton). 1974.
22. Elie Wiesel (Molly Abramowitz). 1974.
23. Paul Laurence Dunbar (Eugene W. Metcalf, Jr.). 1975.
24. Henry James (Beatrice Ricks). 1975.
25. Robert Frost (Lentricchia & Lentricchia). 1976.
26. Sherwood Anderson (Douglas G. Rogers). 1976.
27. Iris Murdoch and Muriel Spark (Tominaga & Schneidermeyer). 1976.
28. John Ruskin (Kirk H. Beetz). 1976.
29. Georges Simenon (Trudee Young). 1976.
30. George Gordon, Lord Byron (Oscar José Santucho). 1976.
31. John Barth (Richard Vine). 1977.
32. John Hawkes (Carol A. Hryciw). 1977.
33. William Everson (Bartlett & Campo). 1977.
34. May Sarton (Lenora Blouin). 1978.
35. Wilkie Collins (Kirk H. Beetz). 1978.
36. Sylvia Plath (Lane & Stevens). 1978.
37. E.B. White (A.J. Anderson). 1978.
38. Henry Miller (Lawrence J. Shifreen). 1979.
39. Ralph Waldo Emerson (Jeanetta Boswell). 1979.
40. James Dickey (Jim Elledge). 1979.

A New Steinbeck Bibliography:

1971-1981

by

TETSUMARO HAYASHI

Scarecrow Author Bibliographies, No. 64

The Scarecrow Press, Inc.
Metuchen, N.J., & London
1983

Library of Congress Cataloging in Publication Data
Hayashi, Tetsumaro.
    A new Steinbeck bibliography: 1971-1981.

    Includes index.
    1. Steinbeck, John, 1902-1968--Bibliography.
I. Title.
Z8839.4.H314   Suppl.   016.813'52   82-24077
[PS3537.T3234]
ISBN 0-8108-1610-5

Copyright © 1983 by Tetsumaro Hayashi

Manufactured in the United States of America

Dedicated to

ROBERT DEMOTT

and

JOHN DITSKY

as a token of esteem, friendship, and gratitude.

CONTENTS

PREFACE

I have long felt an obligation to provide a revised, up-dated, and improved bibliography for the general public, and especially for reference librarians, students, teachers, and scholars who have used my A New Steinbeck Bibliography (1929-1971) in the past ten years. This obligation is espe-cially strong because I have learned a great deal more about Steinbeck from senior scholars as well as emerging younger scholars in the years since 1971, a period that has witnessed explosive activities in research and writing about Steinbeck here and abroad. This new bibliography, 1971-1981, covers only ten years, but the new printed material is almost half that published in the previous forty years (1929-1971). Given this enormous interest in Steinbeck, I felt it necessary to record all the known worthy criticism published from 1971 to 1981 for the benefit of students and scholars of Steinbeck.

Today no student of Steinbeck's literature is unaware of the uninterrupted flow of scholarship that attests both to Steinbeck's perpetual appeal and to his richness; yet this same criticism often seems vast, dazzling, and even chaotic. Con-sequently, students and scholars always need a concise and functional Steinbeck bibliography--a guide that provides a sense of order and cohesiveness to Steinbeck criticism. My only hope is that I have provided this needed tool.

In principle I have followed The Chicago Manual of Style (University of Chicago Press), but I have simplified or revised its system whenever I thought it beneficial or sensible to the users of this bibliography.

Admittedly, this bibliography is selective rather than exhaustive. My controlling principle was to include only important critical sources, published or reprinted in English, on Steinbeck and his literature from 1971 to 1981, although I also took the liberty of including some significant sources published in 1982. Most of the primary and critical items included here were published in the United States; however, if I thought items from other countries might be of particular interest or benefit to some, I included those foreign sources as well.

I have made the following revisions and improvements on A New Steinbeck Bibliography (1929-1971):

(1) OMISSIONS: I have omitted "Verse" because the identification of Steinbeck's poems is still controversial; also most "Excerpts" and "Adaptations" since I believe they are not the major objectives of Steinbeck studies; and "Poems about Steinbeck" and "Audio-Visual Material" because the subjects belong not to Steinbeck criticism but to ephemeral categories.

(2) COMBINATION/SIMPLIFICATION: "Film Reviews" are listed under "Reviews," a category which now includes not only book reviews but also drama, movie, opera, and TV-film reviews.

(3) SEPARATE ENTRIES: I separated "Criticism" ("Articles and Essays Published in Journals, Magazines, and Books") from "Biographies" because "Biographies" should be treated differently from critical assessments of Steinbeck's works. By the same token, I separated "Criticism" from "Reviews."

(4) ADDITIONS: "Surveys of Steinbeck Criticism," "Steinbeck Monograph Series," "Proceedings of Steinbeck Conferences," and "Journals: Special Steinbeck Issues" have been added because each one of these sources renders a unique informational service.

(5) SELECTIVITY: I have included more selected sources in this reference guide than I did in 1973. I have also emphasized the following: a) the English-language critical sources, especially published in the United States; b) more scholarly and teaching-oriented sources; c) published sources--with one exception, "Dissertations"; d) critical sources rather than reviews of critical sources; and e) informational items.

ACKNOWLEDGMENTS

While compiling A New Steinbeck Bibliography: 1971-1981, I have accumulated a debt of gratitude to a number of people and institutions. Although it is impossible for me to list all of them, the following especially have earned my gratitude and appreciation.

I am grateful to Robert DeMott of Ohio University for endorsing my bibliography so enthusiastically in his Introduction. I also deeply appreciate Richard F. Peterson of Southern Illinois University and John Ditsky of the University of Windsor, Canada, for their invaluable advice.

My sincere thanks are due to the editors, compilers, and publishers of those reference books and bibliographical guides included in the sections of "Bibliographies" and "A Selected List of Standard Reference Books Consulted" for their invaluable information. I also wish to thank those incredibly helpful librarians at the Alexander M. Bracken Library of Ball State University, the Indiana University Libraries, Bloomington, Indiana, and the Library of Congress in Washington, D. C. My special appreciation goes to all of my sponsors at Ball State University, but most notably to Dr. Daryl B. Adrian, Dr. Michael C. Gemignani, and Mr. Donald N. Butera for their continued support of my work as teacher, scholar, editor, and advisor at Ball State University, and to my secretaries, Miss April Mercer and Miss Diane Zolper, for their conscientious typing job. The following scholars and friends were helpful in identifying a variety of important critical sources on Steinbeck: Preston Beyer, Ann D'Amico, Maurice Dunbar, Warren French, Reloy Garcia, Thomas J. Moore, Robert E. Morsberger, Anne-Marie and Edwin F. Schmitz, Donald L. Siefker, Juanita J. Smith, and others. I am especially indebted to such outstanding bibliographies and catalogues as those by Adrian H. Goldstone-John R. Payne (1974), John Gross-Lee Richard Hayman (1970), Bradford Morrow (1980), and Susan F. Riggs (1980).

It is to these scholars, librarians, secretaries, publishers, sponsors, and friends that I wish to express my profound gratitude.

Tetsumaro Hayashi
Muncie, Indiana
August 17, 1982

KEY TO ABBREVIATIONS

AL	American Literature
Cf	Confer
DAI	Dissertation Abstracts International
ed.; eds.	edited by
f	film
G of W	The Grapes of Wrath
JML	Journal of Modern Literature
JS	John Steinbeck
KAL	Kyushu American Literature (Japan)
LV	The Long Valley
MFS	Modern Fiction Studies
MLA	The Modern Language Association of America
N. B.	Nota bene (note well!)
n. p.	no page number given or identified
n. p. p.	no publication place given or identified
n. v.	no volume number given or identified
PH	The Pastures of Heaven
PMLA	Publications of the Modern Language Association of America
PS	The Portable Steinbeck
Q	Quarterly

R	Review
S's	Steinbeck's
SHC	Steinbeck and His Critics, eds. Tedlock and Wicker, 1956.
SJS	San Jose Studies
SMS	Steinbeck Monograph Series
SQ	Steinbeck Quarterly
SR	Saturday Review
TCL	Twentieth Century Literature
TLS	Times Literary Supplement (London, England)
WAL	Western American Literature
WOD	The Winter of Our Discontent

Note: "No entry" has been used to replace a deleted item whose identity is questionable or whose publication date was found to be prior to 1971, and therefore out of the range of this supplement.

1902   John Ernst Steinbeck born February 27, in Salinas, California, the third of four children, the only son.

1919   Graduated from Salinas High School, a good student and athlete.

1920   Began intermittent attendance at Stanford University.

1924   First publication: "Fingers of Cloud" and "Adventures in Arcademy," two stories in The Stanford Spectator (February and June).

1925   Left Stanford permanently without a degree. Went to New York City and worked as both construction laborer and reporter for The American (newspaper).

1926   Returned to California. Humorous verses published in Stanford Lit: 1) "If Eddie Guest Had Written the Book of Job: Happy Birthday"; 2) "If John A. Weaver Had Written Keats' Sonnets in the American Language: On Looking at a New Book by Harold Bell Wright"; 3) "Atropos: Study of a Very Feminine Obituary Editor."

1929   First novel, Cup of Gold, published by Robert M. McBride, New York.

1930   Married Carol Henning and began residence in Pacific Grove. First met Edward F. Ricketts, marine biologist and Steinbeck's "artistic conscience." Began permanent association with McIntosh & Otis, his literary agent.

1932   Moved to Los Angeles in summer. The Pastures of Heaven published by Brewer, Warren & Putnam, New York.

1933   Returned to Pacific Grove early in the year. To a God Unknown published by Robert O. Ballou, New York. Two stories, the first two parts of The Red Pony ("The Gift" and "The Great Mountains") published in North American Review in November and December (later included in LV).

1934   Olive Hamilton Steinbeck, John's mother, died in February. "The Murder" selected as an O. Henry Prize Story and published in O. Henry Prize Stories. "The Raid" published in North American Review (both in LV). Ben Abramson brings The Pastures of Heaven and To a God Unknown to the attention of Pascal Covici.

1935   Tortilla Flat published by Covici-Friede, New York, bringing immediate fame and financial success. Won the Commonwealth Club of California Gold Medal.

1936   In Dubious Battle and "Saint Katy the Virgin" published. Won the California Novel of 1936 Prize for the novel. Moved to Los Gatos, California. His father, John Ernst Steinbeck, died in May. A series of eight articles, "The Harvest Gypsies," published in San Francisco News in October (5-12). Trip to Mexico this year.

1937   Of Mice and Men published in February and chosen by the Book-of-the-Month Club. Went to New York and Pennsylvania to work on stage version, which was produced at Music Box Theatre in New York in November and won Drama Critics' Circle Silver Plaque for that season. Chosen one of the ten outstanding young men of the year. First three parts of The Red Pony published. First trip to Europe. Later in year, went to California from Oklahoma with migrants. "The Promise" and "The Ears of Johnny Bear" published in Esquire (September 3; later in LV). "The Chrysanthemums" published in Harper's (October).

1938   The Long Valley (Viking Press, N. Y.)--including
fourth part of The Red Pony--and Their Blood Is
Strong, a pamphlet reprint of "The Harvest Gypsies"
plus an epilogue, published. "The Harness" published in Atlantic Monthly (LV).

1939   The Grapes of Wrath published. National Institute
of Arts and Letters membership given.

1940   The Grapes of Wrath won 1) Pulitzer Prize; 2) American Booksellers Association Award; and 3) Social
Work Today Award. With Edward F. Ricketts went
to Gulf of California on the "Western Flyer" to col-
lect marine invertebrates, March-April. Filmed
The Forgotten Village in Mexico (the book published
in 1941). The Grapes of Wrath (1939) filmed. Of
Mice and Men (1937) filmed.

1941   The Forgotten Village and Sea of Cortez (with Ed
Ricketts) published. "How Edith McGillcuddy Met
R. L. Stevenson" published in Harper's Magazine
(later in Portable Steinbeck).

1942   Separation and interlocutory divorce from Carol Henning. The Moon Is Down (novel) published. Bombs
Away written for Army Air Corps. Tortilla Flat
filmed.

1943   Married Gwyndolen Conger in March and began residence in New York. Spent several months in European war zone as correspondent for New York Herald
Tribune. The Moon Is Down filmed. The Moon Is
Down (play) published. The Portable Steinbeck published with a foreword by Pascal Covici.

1944   His first son, Thomas, born. Wrote film story (unpublished) for Lifeboat, 20th Century-Fox.

1945   Cannery Row published. The Red Pony republished
with fourth chapter, "The Leader of the People."
"The Pearl of the World" (same as The Pearl) appeared in Woman's Home Companion in December.
"A Medal for Benny" (Paramount) filmed. Bought
home in New York.

1946   Won the King Haakon (Norway) Liberty Cross for The
Moon Is Down. A filmscript, "A Medal for Benny,"

published. John IV born, his second son. New edition of The Portable S.

1947   Trip to Russia with Robert Capa, August-September.
The Wayward Bus published. The Pearl published
and filmed. Norwegian Award for The Moon Is Down.
The Wayward Bus selected as the Book-of-the-Month
Club book.

1948   Elected to American Academy of Arts and Letters.
Divorced from Gwyn Conger. A Russian Journal
(with Robert Capa), an account of his trip to Russia,
published. Edward F. Ricketts died. A short story,
"Miracle of Tepayac," published in Collier's.

1949   The Red Pony filmed. A short story, "His Father,"
published in Reader's Digest.

1950   Burning Bright (play and novel) published. Married
to Elaine Scott in December. Viva Zapata! (20th
Century-Fox) filmed.

1951   The Log from the Sea of Cortez published, containing
introduction and narrative from Sea of Cortez and
biography of Edward F. Ricketts. Burning Bright
(play) published. Part of summer in Nantucket.

1952   East of Eden published. Sent reports to Collier's
from Europe (May-September).

1954   Sweet Thursday published.

1955   Pipe Dream (Richard Rodgers and Oscar Hammerstein
II musical comedy based on Sweet Thursday) pro-
duced. Editorials for Saturday Review. East of
Eden (1952) filmed. Bought house in Sag Harbor,
Long Island, for summers.

1956   The O. Henry Award for "Affair at 7, Rue de M. ---."

1957   The Short Reign of Pippin IV published. The Wayward Bus (1947) filmed. Trip to Europe with sister,
Mary Dekker, and wife. Beginning of serious research into Malory and the Morte d'Arthur, including
first trip into "Malory country."

1958   Once There Was a War, a collection of wartime dispatches, published. June in England; more Malory explorations; involved with Malory scholarship with Dr. Eugène Vinaver.

1959   Eleven months in England, living in Discove Cottage near Bruton, Somerset and working on modernization of Morte.

1960   A three-month trip by truck around U.S.A. Work on Morte put off till "later."

1961   The Winter of Our Discontent, his last novel, published. The Book-of-the-Month Club selected The Winter of Our Discontent. "Flight" (a short story) filmed in San Francisco and independently produced. Traveled ten months in Europe. In November, had first heart attack.

1962   Travels with Charley published. Received Nobel Prize for Literature in December.

1963   Cultural Exchange trip behind Iron Curtain: Steinbecks and Edward Albee.

1964   An Annual Paperback of the Year Award, a plaque for his Travels with Charley (Bantam), and the John F. Kennedy Memorial Library Trusteeship given. Won a Press Medal of Freedom and a United States (Presidential) Medal of Freedom. Death of Pascal Covici in October.

1965   Travel in London and Paris at first of year. Death of sister, Mary Dekker.

1966   America and Americans published. Articles ("Letters to Alicia") for Newsday (1966-67). Trips to Israel and Southeast Asia writing for Newsday. [The John Steinbeck Society of America was founded in January at Kent State University by Tetsumaro Hayashi and Preston Beyer.]

1967   Home from Asia, May 1. In autumn, a back operation and spinal fusion.

1968   Suffered from coronary disease and died of a heart attack in New York City on December 20. [The Steinbeck Quarterly began to be published in February under T. Hayashi's editorship at Kent State University (originally entitled the Steinbeck Newsletter).]

1969   The Journal of a Novel posthumously published in December. [The Steinbeck Conference held in May at the University of Connecticut under the direction of John Seelye.]

1970   New edition of The Portable Steinbeck, revised by Pascal Covici, Jr.

1971   [The Steinbeck Monograph Series began to be published under T. Hayashi's general editorship at Ball State University.]

1975   Steinbeck: A Life in Letters, eds. Elaine Steinbeck and Robert Wallsten, and Steinbeck's Viva Zapata!, ed. Robert E. Morsberger, were published by the Viking Press.

1976   Steinbeck's The Acts of King Arthur and His Noble Knights, ed. Chase Horton, was published by Farrar, Straus and Giroux in New York.

INTRODUCTION

Nearly twenty years ago, when I did my first work on Steinbeck (a paltry undergraduate thesis), there were only a few contemporary critical books available--Tedlock and Wicker's Steinbeck and His Critics, Warren French's John Steinbeck, Joseph Fontenrose's John Steinbeck: An Introduction and Interpretation, F. W. Watt's Steinbeck, and, of course, Peter Lisca's The Wide World of John Steinbeck. Except for Lisca's book, doubly valuable for its "Working Checklist of Steinbeck's Published Work," a comprehensive bibliography of work by and about Steinbeck did not exist. Fortunately, the situation improved shortly afterwards when the special Steinbeck number of Modern Fiction Studies, with Beebe and Bryer's "Criticism of John Steinbeck: A Selected Checklist," appeared in 1965. With these two items it was at least possible to see a larger picture of Steinbeck and, as Ted Hayashi later did, to imagine bringing that picture even more clearly into focus. In the years since 1965, and especially in the past decade, Steinbeck publications have--like everything else in American literary studies--proliferated so rapidly that they now constitute a small industry. More than ever before, accurate bibliographical resources (I mean bibliography in its largest sense, regardless of format, arrangement, or purpose) are absolutely necessary.

Ted Hayashi has been at the forefront of that critical concern, not only as founder and editor of the indispensable Steinbeck Quarterly and the Steinbeck Monograph Series, but even before that with his original Steinbeck bibliography in 1967, then with his corrected and enlarged version, A New Steinbeck Bibliography, 1929-1971 (1973), and now with this much needed supplement. In fact, the general state of Steinbeck bibliography has improved immensely in the past ten years. Steinbeck is one of those writers who have been followed with enormous enthusiasm by teachers, scholars, book collectors, and librarians; the results of their diverse (but equally passionate) attentions have permanently altered Steinbeck studies for the better. Today, the person equipped with Hayashi's books, as well as Goldstone and Payne's valuable descriptive bibliography, Susan Riggs' catalogue of the John Steinbeck Collection at Stanford University, the Gross and Hayman guide to the Steinbeck Collection at the Salinas Public Library, and Bradford Morrow's sale catalogue of Harry Valentine's Steinbeck collection is in a position--perhaps really for the first time--to realize the true range and scope of writing by and about John Steinbeck.

These and other breakthroughs in bibliography have been paralleled by--and in some cases have actually helped form-- new critical approaches to Steinbeck's work. Enlarging the boundaries of Steinbeck's canon has created a correspondingly healthy curiosity in many critics and has generated a variety of fascinating perspectives. (I think immediately of the late Lawrence William Jones' study of Steinbeck as a fabulist, Richard Astro's influential book on Steinbeck and Ed Ricketts, and Robert Morsberger's work on Steinbeck's filmscripts.) Even a quick glance at this new volume will reveal an increased focus on Steinbeck's later fiction. Fewer and fewer critics are willing to accept the harsh formalist decrees about Steinbeck's decline as an artist in the 1940's, and consequently such books as Cannery Row, East of Eden and The Winter of Our Discontent have started to attract their share of responsible investigations. Part of that same reaction against categorizing Steinbeck as some sort of empirical journalist, proletarian naturalist or glorified sociologist is also apparent in the number and quality of writings on his mythic strategies (chiefly on the influence of Carl Jung, whose books Steinbeck knew first-hand). Then, too, because of the publication of several important selections of his letters, and with the increasing availability of primary documents at various institutional collections, the recent surge of articles, essays, books, and dissertations on Steinbeck (witness particularly the work of Martha Cox, Mark Govoni, Robin Mitchell, Roy Simmonds, and Agatha TeMaat) are often more informed, original, and stimulating than their predecessors.

Yet, despite this expanded treatment of Steinbeck, there are still whole areas that need attention. On the primary side, a comprehensive scholarly edition of Steinbeck's correspondence, an annotated edition of his journals, and a representative selection of his non-fictional prose (there is one published in Japan, but not in America), including his "Letters to Alicia," are all still lacking. On the secondary side, we need an annotated bibliography of criticism, a chronological collection of newspaper and periodical reviews of his writings, studies of his relationship with critics and reviewers whose work he generally trusted (Lewis Gannett and Joseph Henry Jackson, for instance), a catalogue of his manuscripts and letters, and much more on his theory of fiction (already admirably addressed by Jackson Benson, John Ditsky, and Warren French). Finally, I hope my forthcoming book Steinbeck's Reading (it includes nearly 1000 books Steinbeck read, owned, or borrowed) will make possible a sustained and vigorous investigation of the numerous sources he drew upon in his own writings. More to the point, a sound bibliography of primary and secondary entries is the starting place for all of these ventures; otherwise, we go on working in the dark, doomed to perpetuate the same misconceptions endlessly.

Until fairly recently, the tendency to treat only Steinbeck's most accessible publications has led to considerable neglect of his fugitive items. Yet these, too, have an important function if we are going to understand the intricacies of his career. The popular notion that Steinbeck read little or no contemporary fiction is strongly controverted by his enthusiastic letter to John Hargrave, author of Summer Time Ends, an enormous experimental novel in the Joycean tradition (see entry no. 689). And consider André Gide, whose sensibility also differed from Steinbeck's. We know that Gide praised Steinbeck's fiction, particularly In Dubious Battle, but it might come as a surprise to learn that Steinbeck considered Gide's The Counterfeiters "one of the greatest novels" he had ever read (see "Un Grand Romancier de Notre Temps," entry no. 134a). Anyone interested in Steinbeck's formative experience should become familiar with "Preface" to the last edition of Edith Mirrielees' Story Writing (see entry no. 191), for she had been his creative writing instructor at Stanford and, by his own admission, one of the greatest teachers he ever had. (The crystalline quality of his Long Valley stories certainly owes something to her advice.) While Steinbeck could be playful about some of his literary pronouncements, as in his introduction to Al Capp's The World of Li'l Abner (see entry no. 151), he could also produce wonderful brief pieces. The most succinct statement I know of his writing method occurs in a letter quoted in the "Foreword" of Fred Allen's Much Ado About Me (see entry no. 127), and one of the loveliest appraisals he ever made about the fiction writer's task is "In Awe of Words" (see entry no. 149a). To overlook any of these items means missing resonant additions to the Steinbeck canon.

Even though in his early years Steinbeck frequently disparaged the bibliographic life, he did believe, as he says in "Some Random and Randy Thoughts on Books" (see entry no. 206), that books are "sacred." By the time he began writing his modernized version of Sir Thomas Malory's Morte d'Arthur in the late 1950's, Steinbeck had immersed himself so thoroughly in his research (hundreds of books read, bought, and borrowed) that he not only became an accomplished scholar of the subject (praised by no less an authority than Eugène Vinaver), but, with Chase Horton's help at Washington Square Book Store, became a zealous bibliographer as well.

With that turn of events in mind, it is tempting to think that Steinbeck would have approved of Ted Hayashi's bibliographical efforts. Getting it right, seeing the whole picture--these are propositions Steinbeck adhered to throughout his life; perhaps more than anyone else in the past fifteen years, Ted Hayashi has made it possible for the rest of us to live up to those demanding standards and add what we can to the constantly evolving record.

Robert DeMott
Ohio University

A. FICTION (NOVELS)

N. B.: For current editions in print, check the latest Books in Print (New York: Bowker) or Paperbound Books in Print (New York: Bowker) or Cumulative Book Index (New York: Wilson).

1. The Acts of King Arthur and His Noble Knights, ed. Chase Horton. New York: Farrar, Straus and Giroux, 1976.

2. Burning Bright. New York: Viking Press, 1950.

3. Cannery Row. New York: Viking Press, 1945.

4. Cup of Gold: A Life of Henry Morgan, Buccaneer, with Occasional References to History. New York: Robert M. McBride, 1929.

5. East of Eden. New York: Viking Press, 1952.

6. The Grapes of Wrath. New York: Viking Press, 1939.

7. In Dubious Battle. New York: Covici-Friede, 1936.

   [99 deluxe copies, numbered and signed by the author.]

8. The Long Valley. New York: Viking Press, 1938.

Including the following short stories:
"The Chrysanthemums"
"The White Quail"
"Flight"
"The Snake"
"The Breakfast"
"The Raid"
"The Harness"
"The Vigilante"
"Johnny Bear"
"The Murder"
"St. Katy the Virgin"
The Red Pony:
   "The Gift"
   "The Great Mountains"
   "The Promise"
   "The Leader of the People."

9.   The Moon Is Down. New York: Viking Press, 1942.

[700 copies bound in paper for distribution exclusively to booksellers.]

10.   Of Mice and Men. New York: Covici-Friede, 1937.

[2,500 copies were printed. Page 9, lines 2-3 from the bottom of the page, read "and only moved because the heavy hands were/pendula." This was removed in later printings. Text of the Book-of-the-Month-Club copies is identical to the second printing.]

11.   The Pastures of Heaven. New York: Brewer, Warren and Putnam, 1932.

12.   The Pearl. New York: Viking Press, 1947.

13.   The Red Pony. New York: Covici-Friede, 1937.

Set in monotype Italian Oldstyle and printed on handmade La Garde paper; 699 numbered copies were printed by the Pynson Printers of New York under the supervision of Elmer Adler, each copy signed by the author, September, 1937.
I.   "The Gift"
II.   "The Great Mountains"
III.   "The Promise" (The 1945 ed. includes IV).
IV.   "The Leader of the People"
[Included in LV in 1938.]

14. The Short Reign of Pippin IV: A Fabrication. New
    York: Viking Press, 1957.

15. Sweet Thursday. New York: Viking Press, 1954.

16. To a God Unknown. New York: Robert O. Ballou,
    1933.

17. Tortilla Flat. Illustrated by Ruth Gannett. New York:
    Covici-Friede, 1935.

    [500 copies were printed as prepublication copies.
    Later editions so indicated on copyright page.]

18. The Wayward Bus. New York: Viking Press, 1947.

19. The Winter of Our Discontent. New York: Viking
    Press, 1961.

B. FICTION (SHORT STORIES)

20. "Adventures in Arcademy: A Journey into the Ridicu-
    lous," Stanford Spectator, 2 (June 1924), 279, 291.

21. "Affair at 7, Rue de M. ---," Prize Stories 1956: The
    O. Henry Awards, eds. Paul Engle and Hansford
    Martin. Garden City, N.Y.: Doubleday, 1956. Re-
    printed from Harper's Bazaar (April 1955), 258-65.
    Also in Knight, 5 (September 1966), 26-29.

22. "Breakfast," Progressive Weekly, (n.v.) (May 6, 1939),
    [n.p.]. Also in LV and PS as well as in Pacific
    Weekly, 15 (November 9, 1936), [n.p.]. Also in
    Turning Point: Fourteen Great Tales of Daring and
    Decision, ed. George Bennett. New York: Dell,
    1956. pp. 174-77.

23. "The Chrysanthemums," American Literature, eds.
    Richard Poirier and William L. Vance. Boston:
    Little, Brown, 1970. II, 840-48.

    Fiction for Composition by Bert C. Bach and Gor-
    don Browning. Chicago: Scott, Foresman, 1968.
    pp. 262, 276-86.

    50 Best American Short Stories: 1915-1965, ed.

Martha Foley. London: MacGibbon and Kee, 1966.
pp. 203-13.

Harper's, 175 (October 1937), 513-19. Also in
LV, PS, 1938.

24. "Cutting Loose, " in collaboration with Michael Ratcliffe.
Encore, ed. Leonard Russell. London: Michael
Joseph, 1963.

25. "Danny and His Friends, " PS and A Treasury of Friendship, comp. and ed. Ralph L. Woods. New York:
David McKay, 1957.

26. "Death of Grampa, " from The Grapes of Wrath at the
Flood: The Human Drama as Seen by Modern American Novelists, ed. Ann Watkins. New York: Harper, 1946.

27. "Death Shall Be Paid, " PS.

28. "Dust, " Reading I've Liked, ed. C. Fadiman. New York:
Simon and Schuster, 1945.

29. "The Ears of Johnny Bear, " The Bedside Esquire, pp.
379-93.

Esquire, 8 (September 1937), 195-200; in LV as
"Johnny Bear. " Also in The Bedside Esquire, ed.
A. Gingrich. New York: Tudor, 1937.

30. "Edith McGillcuddy, " Lilliput, 12 (April 1943), 285-90;
The 1943 Saturday Book, ed. Leonard Russell. London: Huntington, 1942. pp. 189-99.

31. "The Elf in Algiers, " Pause to Wonder, eds. Marjorie
Fischer and Rolfe Humphries. Garden City, N. Y.:
Sun Dial Press, 1947; also New York: Julian Mess-
ner, Inc. , 1944. pp. 401-03 [Also in Once There
Was a War as "The Story of an Elf, " pp. 190-94.]

32. "Fingers of Cloud: A Satire on College Protervity, "
Stanford Spectator, 2 (February, 1924), 149, 161-64
(Author's name printed John E. Steinback). Also in
Stanford Writers, 1891-1941, ed. Violet L. Shue. pp.
103-08; Dramatists Alliance, Stanford University.
Limited to 300 copies.

33. "Flight," Fiction Form and Experience: 30 Stories with
Essays, ed. William M. Jones. Lexington, Mass.:
Heath, 1969. pp. 147-61.

An Introduction to Short Fiction and Criticism, eds.
Emil Hurtik and Robert Yarber. Waltham, Mass.:
Xerox College Publishing, 1971. pp. 96-107.

LV and PS. Also in Adventures in American Literature, eds. R. B. Inglis, et al. New York: Harcourt Brace, 1951. Also in Introduction to the Short
Story: Study Materials, eds. W. Boynton and May-
nard Mack. New York: Hayden Book Co., 1965.

The Narrative Impulse: Short Stories for Analysis,
eds. Mary Purcell and Robert C. Wylder. New York:
Odyssey Press, 1963. pp. 166-87.

Short Story Masterpieces, eds. Robert Penn Warren and Albert Erskine. New York: Dell, 1954.
pp. 454-74.

34. "Free Ride to Monterey," Argosy, 4 (March 1943), 69-
76.

35. "The Gift," LV, PS, and The Red Pony. Also in The
Pocket Reader. New York: Pocket Books, 1941.

36. "The Great Mountains," North American R, 236 (December 1933), 492-500. Also in LV and PS and Two and
Twenty, A Collection of Short Stories, ed. R. H. Sin-
gleton. New York: St. Martin's, 1962. pp. 236-38;
236-38 contain some biobibliographical information
about S. Also in Accents, eds. Robert C. Pooley,
et al. Chicago: Scott, Foresman, 1965. pp. 584-
91.

37. "The Hanging at San Quentin," Avon, No. 20, 1945.

38. "The Harness," Argosy, 6 (June 1945), 15-25.

Atlantic, 161 (June 1938), 741-49. Also in LV
and PS.

50 Great American Short Stories, ed. Milton Crane.
New York: Bantam, 1966.

39. "His Father," Reader's Digest, 55 (October 1949), 10-12 [British Version].

   Reader's Digest, 55 (September 1949), 19-21.

40. "How Edith McGillcuddy Met R. L. Stevenson," Harper's, 183 (August 1941), 252-58. Also in PS and Scholastic, 44 (April 24, 1944), 21-22. Also in The Best American Short Stories of 1942, ed. Martha Foley. Boston: Houghton Mifflin, 1952; and The Best Short Stories of 1942, O. Henry Memorial Stories, ed. H. Brickell. New York: Literary Guild, 1942.

   Strand Magazine, 103 (June 1942), 16-23.

   How Edith McGillcuddy Met R. L. Stevenson. Cleveland: Rowfant Club, 1943.

41. "How Mr. Hogan Robbed a Bank," Atlantic, 197 (March 1956), 58-61. Also in Working with Prose, ed. Otto Reinert. New York: Harcourt, Brace, 1959. pp. 20-30.

42. "Johnny Bear," Argosy, 1 (New Series) (January 1941), 97-111.

   LV [See "The Ears of Johnny Bear"]. Also in Great Tales of the Far West, No. 88. New York: Lion Library, 1956.

   (From LV) Pultizer Prize Reader (The Popular Living Classics Library), eds. Leo Hamalian and E. L. Volpe (Introduction by Leon Edel) (No. 95-172). New York: Popular Library, 1961.

43. "The King Snake and the Rattler," Brief, 66 (April 1953), 22-27.

44. "The Leader of the People," American Literature. Boston: Heath, 1969. II, 3231-50.

   American Literature Survey, eds. Milton R. Stern and Seymour L. Gross. New York: Viking, 1962 (1972). IV, 152-67.

   Argosy, 20 (August 1936), 99-106.

Insight I: Analyses of American Literature, eds.
John V. Hagopian and Martin Dolch. Frankfurt:
Hirschgroben, 1962. pp. 231-35.

LV and PS. Also in The Golden Argosy. New
York: Dial Press, 1955. Also in The Pocket
Book of Modern American Short Stories, ed. Philip
Van Doren Stern. New York: Pocket Books, 1943.
Also in This Is My Best Edition, ed. Whit Burnett.
New York: Dial Press, 1942. Also in The United
States in Literature, eds. Walter Blair, et al. Chi-
cago: Scott, Foresman, 1963. pp. 417-86.

Youth and Maturity: 20 Short Stories, ed. James
Coulos. New York: Macmillan, 1970. pp. 319-30.

45. "Lilli Marlene" [from Once There Was a War (pp. 130-
33)], The Best of the Diners' Club Magazine, eds.
Matty Simmonds and Sam Boal. New York: Regent
American Pub., 1962. p. 322.

46. "The Lonesome Vigilante," The Bedside Esquire. pp.
307-12.

Best of the Bedside Esquire, ed. Arnold Gingrich.
London: Strato Publications, 1954. pp. 189-95.

Esquire, 6 (October 1936), 35; 186A-186B. Also
in LV as "The Vigilante" [See "Vigilante"].

The Esquire Treasury, ed. Arnold Gingrich. London: Heinemann, 1954. pp. 99-103.

47. "The Miracle," Argosy, 10 (April 1949), 97-103.

48. "Miracle of Tepayac," Collier's, 122 (December 25,
1948), 22-23.

49. "Molly Morgan," in PS. Also in Avon, No. 31, 1946.

50. "The Murder," The American Tradition in Literature,
eds. Scully Bradley, et al. New York: Norton,
1967. II, 1506-26.

Argosy, 2 (New Series) (March 1941), 31-40.

North American R, 237 (April 1934), 305-12. Also

in LV and O. Henry Prize Stories of 1934. New York: Doubleday, Doran, 1934. Also in The Bedside Tales, introduced by Peter Arno. New York: William Penn Pub., 1945. Also in Lovat Dickson's Magazine (England) 3 (October 1934), 442-56.

51. "Nothing for Himself," Continent's End: A Collection of California Writing, ed. Joseph Henry Jackson. New York: McGraw-Hill, 1944.

52. Nothing So Monstrous. New York: Pynson Printers, 1936.

[A reprint of the Junius Maltby story from The Pastures of Heaven with illustration by Donald McKay and an epilogue by the author written for this edition of 370 unnumbered copies. Also in Modern Age Books. Avon (Short Story Monthly), No. 20, 1945.]

53. "Over the Hill," Half-a-Hundred: Tales by Great American Writers, ed. Charles Grayson. Toronto: Blakiston, 1945. Also, Philadelphia: Blakiston, 1945, 450-52.

54. "The Pearl of the World," Woman's Home Companion, 72 (December 1945), 177ff. [See The Pearl].

55. "The Promise," Harper's, 175 (August 1937), 243-52. Also in LV and PS. Part III of The Red Pony: O. Henry Prize Stories of 1938. New York: Doubleday, Doran, 1938.

56. "The Raid," Modern American Short Stories, eds. Alan Steele and Joan Hancock. Penguin Books, No. 116 (Forces Book Club Edition), 1942. pp. 65-75.

North American R, 238 (October 1934), 229-305. Also in LV.

Stories of Our Time, ed. Douglas R. Barnes. London: Harrap, 1963. pp. 120-33.

57. "The Red Pony," Reading I've Liked, ed. Clifton Fadiman. London: Hamilton, 1946. pp. 437-95 ["The Leader of the People" is omitted].

"The Red Pony--Part I: 'The Gift,' "Stories from The

Quarto, ed. Leonard Brown. New York: Scribner's, 1963. pp. 142-53.

58. "Reunion at the Quiet Hotel," Evening Standard, January 25, 1958. p. 9.

59. Saint Katy the Virgin. New York: Covici-Friede, 1936.

   [199 numbered copies, signed by the author; also in LV.]

60. "The Short-Short Story of Mankind," Penguin Science Fiction, ed. Brian Aldiss. Harmondsworth: Penguin Books, 1961. pp. 51-57.

   The Permanent Playboy, ed. Ray Russell. New York: Crown, 1959. p. 325.

61. "The Snake," Monterey Beacon, 1 (June 22, 1953), 10-14; also in LV; Great American Short Stories, eds. Wallace and Mary Stegner. New York: Dell, 1957.

62. "A Snake of One's Own," The Bedside Esquire, ed. Arnold Gingrich. New York: Tudor Pub., 1954; London: Heinemann, 1941. pp. 530-38. Also in The Best, a Quarterly Magazine, "a continuing anthology of the world's greatest writing." New York: Macfadden-Bartell Corp. [Winter 1965].

   The Girls from Esquire, ed. Frederic A. Birmingham. London: Arthur Barker, 1953. pp. 18-27.

63. "Sons of Cyrus Trask," Collier's, 130 (July 12, 1952), 14-15, 217.

64. "The Time the Wolves Ate the Vice Principal," '47 The Magazine of the Year, 1 (March 1947), 26-27.

   [An interchapter omitted from Cannery Row.]

65. "Tractored Off," Literature for Our Time: An Anthology for College Freshmen, eds. Leonard Stanley Brown, et al. New York: H. Holt and Co., 1947. Also in America in Literature, ed. Tremaine McDowell. Madison, Wisc.: F. S. Crofts and Co., for the U.S. Armed Forces Institute, 1944.

66. "The Tractors," Our Lives: American Labor Stories, ed. Joseph Gaer. New York: Boni and Gaer, 1948.

67. "The Turtle," PS. Also in Reading I've Liked, ed. Clifton Fadiman. New York: Simon and Schuster, 1945.

68. "The Vigilante," LV. See "The Lonesome Vigilante."

69. "The White Quail," American Short Stories, eds. Eugene Current-Garcia and Walton R. Patrick. Chicago: Scott, Foresman, 1964 [n. p.].

   North American R, 239 (March 1935), 204-11. Also in LV and American Short Stories. Chicago: Scott, Foresman and Co., 1952.

C. PLAYS

70. Burning Bright (Acting Edition). New York: Dramatists Play Service, 1951.

71. The Moon Is Down: A Play. New York: Dramatists Play Service, 1942.

72. Of Mice and Men: A Play in Three Acts. New York: Covici-Friede, 1937. Also in Famous American Plays of the 1930s, ed. Harold Clurman. New York: Dell, 1959. pp. 297-394, and Twenty Best Plays of the Modern American Theatre, ed. John Gassner. New York: Crown, 1941. pp. 643-80.

73. Pipe Dream. New York: Viking Press, 1956 [Richard Rodgers/Oscar Hammerstein musical comedy based on Sweet Thursday].

D. FILM STORIES AND SCRIPTS

74. The Forgotten Village. New York: Viking Press, 1941.

75. Lifeboat. Unpublished novel, 1943 (200 pp.) (20th Century Film Corp. , 1944).

76. The Pearl (from his novel). Unpublished script (RKO, 1947).

77. The Red Pony (from his stories). Unpublished script. [Feldman Group Productions and Lewis Milestone Production, 1949].

78. Viva Zapata! Screenplay abridged in Argosy, 33 (February 1952). Based on the Steinbeck-Elia Kazan movie. The pictures were taken on location along the Mexican border; a text, edited by Robert E. Morsberger. New York: Viking Press, 1975.

E. NON-FICTION (BOOKS/BOOKLETS)

79. America and Americans. New York: Viking Press, 1966. Photos by the staff of the Viking Photo Studio.

80. Bombs Away: The Story of a Bomber Team. Written for the U.S. Army Air Forces with 60 photographs by John Swope. New York: Viking Press, 1942.

81. The Log from the Sea of Cortez. New York: Viking Press, 1951. The narrative portion of Sea of Cortez: A Leisurely Journal of Travel and Research, 1941, with a profile "About Ed Ricketts." See Sea of Cortez.

82. Once There Was a War. New York: Viking Press, 1958.

[A collection of S's wartime dispatches to the New York Herald Tribune.]

83. A Russian Journal. New York: Viking Press, 1948. Robert Capa as photographer.

84. Sea of Cortez: A Leisurely Journal of Travel and Research, with Edward F. Ricketts. New York: Viking Press, 1941 [See The Log from the Sea of Cortez.]

85. Their Blood Is Strong (Booklet). San Francisco: Simon J. Lubin Society of California, 1938.

[Pamphlet of articles published in San Francisco News, October 5-12, 1936, as "The Harvest Gypsies".]

Their Blood Is Strong (Booklet). San Francisco: The
Simon J. Lubin Society of California, 1938. Reprinted in A Companion to "The Grapes of Wrath,"
ed. Warren French. New York: Viking Press, 1963.
pp. 53-92.

86. Travels with Charley in Search of America. New York:
Viking Press, 1962.

87. Vanderbilt Clinic (Booklet). New York: Presbyterian
Hospital, 1947.

[An illustrated brochure, with commentary by S.
on the services of the Medical Center and its clinics,
with Victor Kepler as photographer.]

F. NON-FICTION (ARTICLES, ESSAYS,
INTERVIEWS, AND REPORTS)

88. "About Ed Ricketts," Preface to The Log from the Sea
of Cortez. New York: Viking Press, 1951. pp.
vii-lxvii.

89. "The Alien They Couldn't Intern," Daily Express, July
10, 1943. p. 2.

90. "Alliance by Gum," Daily Express, September 13, 1943.
p. 2.

91. "Always Something to Do in Salinas," Holiday, 17 (June
1955), 58ff.

92. A memorial tribute by S. in Pascal Covici 1888-1964.

[Series of tributes to Pascal Covici. Privately
printed. Limited to 500 copies. Not for sale. pp.
19-20.]

93. "Atque Vale," SR, 43 (July 23, 1960), 13.

See also "Blackman's Ironic Burden" (95).

94. "Big Man from Monterey," Manchester Guardian, October 13, 1957. p. 7.

[Interview by W. J. Weatherby.]

95. "Black Man's Ironic Burden," Negro History Bulletin, 24 (April, 1961), 146ff. [Reprint of "Atque Vale."]

96. "Bomber, Our Best Weapon," Science Digest, 14 (July 1943), 61-63.

97. "Bricklaying Piece," Punch, 229 (July 27, 1955), 92.

98. "The Cab Driver Doesn't Give a Hoot," Daily Mail, August 14, 1956.

99. "Camping Is for the Birds" (The Great Camping Debate with Erle Stanley Gardner), Popular Science, 190 (May 1961), 160-161+.

100. "The Case of Arthur Miller," The Armchair Esquire, ed. Arnold Gingrich. London: Heinemann, 1959. pp. 239-42.

101. "Commander Goat, D.S.O.," Daily Express, July 15, 1943. p. 2.

102. "The Common Man at War," Daily Express, June 28, 1943. p. 2.

103. "The Common Man at War 2: When the Saints Go In," Daily Express, June 29, 1943. p. 2.

104. "The Common Man at War 3: This Is Your Target; Knock It Out," Daily Express, June 30, 1943. p. 2.

105. "Contribution to Symposium Entitled 'California: the Exploding State,'" Sunday Times Colour Section, December 16, 1962. p. 2.

106. "Conversation at Sag Harbor," Holiday, 29 (March 1961), 60-61, 129-131, 133.

107. "Critics, Critics Burning Bright," SR, 33 (November 11, 1950), 20-21. Also in SHC. pp. 43-47. Also in Bantam edition (913), 1951. pp. 106-11.

[A statement of S's intention in Burning Bright.]

108. "Critics from a Writer's Viewpoint," SR, 38 (August 27, 1955), 20. Also in SHC, pp. 48-51.

109. "Cutting Loose at 60" (Interview by Michael Ratcliffe), Sunday (London) Times, December 16, 1962. Also in The Sunday Times Book: Encore, eds. Leonard Russell and Michael Joseph, pp. 151-54.

110. "D for Dangerous," McCall's, 85 (October 1957), 57ff.

111. "A Day, a Mood, a Faith in a Spirited Collection of Classic Holiday Messages You Will Long Remember," Good Housekeeping, 165 (1967), 82-83.

112. "The Death of a Racket," SR, 38 (April 2, 1955), 26; Spectator, 6615 (April 8, 1955), 430-31.

113. "Dedication," Journal of American Medical Association, 167 (July 12, 1958), 1388-89. [See "Spivacks Beat the Odds" condensed in Reader's Digest.]

114. Del Monte Recipes. Del Monte, California, 1937.

    Issued by the Del Monte Properties Co. as a promotion piece for the Hotel Del Monte. S's favorite recipe is included among those of other people. [S's article included].

115. "Dichos: The Way of Wisdom," SR, 40 (November 9, 1957), 13.

116. "Discovering the People of Paris," Holiday, 20 (August 1956), 36.

117. Dispatches from the European War Theater appearing in New York Herald Tribune, June 21 to December 10, 1943.

118. "Dover--It Will Bloom Again, Prettier Than Ever," Daily Express, July 9, 1943. p. 2.

119. "Dubious Battle in California," Nation, 143 (September 13, 1936), 302-04.

120. "Duel Without Pistols," Collier's, 130 (August 23, 1952), 13-15, 26ff.

121. "The Easiest Way to Die," SR, 41 (August 23, 1958), 12ff; The SR Sample of Wit and Wisdom, ed. Martin Levin. New York: Simon and Schuster, 1967.

122. Famous Recipes by Famous People, ed. Herbert Cerivin. Illustrated by Sinclair Ross. Published by Sunset Magazine in cooperation with Hotel Del Monte, San Francisco, California. "Of Beef and Men," p. 11.

123. "Fishing in Paris," Punch, 227 (August 25, 1954), 248-49.

    [This article is reprinted in translation under the title "Sur les Bords de l'Oise" as the 8th essay in Un American à New York et à Paris. Paris: Julliard, 1956.]

124. Foreword to Between Pacific Tides. Stanford University Press, 1948.

    [An offprint from the revised edition, issued August 1948, of a work by Edward F. Ricketts and Jack Calvin. Privately printed at the Stanford University Press by Nathan Van Patten.]

125. Foreword to Burning Bright: A Play in Story Form. New York: Viking Press, 1950. pp. 9-13.

126. "Foreword" to Hard-Hitting Songs for Hard-Hit People. New York: Oak Publications, 1967 [n. p.].

127. "Foreword" to Much Ado About Me, by Fred Allen. Boston: Little, Brown, 1956.

128. Foreword to Speeches of Adlai Stevenson, ed. Richard Harrity. New York: Random House, 1952. pp. 5-8.

129. "No entry."

130. "A Game of Hospitality," SR, 40 (April 20, 1957), 24.

131. "Gathering Knowledge," The Treasure Chest, ed. Donald J. Adams. New York: Dutton, 1946. p. 373.

132. "The GI's War....," New York Herald Tribune Weekly Book Review, May 18, 1947. p. 1.

133. "Golden Handcuff: J. S. Writes About San Francisco," San Francisco Examiner, November 23, 1958 [n. p.].

134. "Good Guy--Bad Guy," Punch, 227 (September 22, 1954), 375-78.

134a. "Un Grand Romancier de Notre Temps," Hommage à André Gide, ed. Jean Schlumberger. Paris: La Nouvelle Revue Française, 1951, p. 30.

135. "Green Paradise," Argosy, 17 (May 1956), 41-47.

136. "The Harvest Gypsies," San Francisco News, October 5-12, 1936.

> A series of articles on migrant labor in California:

Chapter		
I.	October 5, 1936	(p. 3)
II.	October 6, 1936	(p. 3)
III.	October 7, 1936	(p. 6)
IV.	October 8, 1936	(p. 16)
V.	October 9, 1936	(p. 14)
VI.	October 10, 1936	(p. 14)
VII.	October 11, 1936	(p. 8)

137. "He Knew What He Wanted," Daily Express, July 24, 1943. p. 2.

138. "Henry Fonda," Harper's Bazaar, [n. v.] (November 1966), 215. Also reprinted in The Fondas: The Films and Careers of Henry, Jane, and Peter (New York: Citadel Press, 1970). pp. 22-25 [S's tribute].

> [On Mohole Project.]

139. "High Drama of Bold Thrust Through Ocean Floor," Life, 50 (April 14, 1961), 110-18.

140. Holloway, David. "J. S. Is Still a Rebel," News Chronicle, June 15, 1957, p. 4 [Interview].

141. "Hostess with the Mostest in the Hall," Daily Mail, August 17, 1956. p. 4.

142. "How to Fish in French," Reader's Digest, 65 (Dec. 1954), 129-31 [Condensed from Punch].

143. "How to Recognize a Candidate," Punch, 229 (August 10, 1955), 146-48.

144. "How to Tell Good Guys from Bad Guys," Reach Out by Marsha Jeffer and Nancy Rayl. Boston: Little Brown, 1972. p. 126-28.

145. "I'll Have a Row in London," Sunday Citizen, December 9, 1962. p. 2

     [Interview with Alan Moray Williams.]

146. "I'll Remember the Thirties," The Thirties: A Time to Remember, ed. Don Congdon. New York: Simon and Schuster, 1962. pp. 23-36. Condensed from Esquire, 103 (June 1960), 23-26.

147. "If You See Me on the Hoe with a PUMA," Daily Mail, September 30, 1959. p. 6.

148. "In Passing, Then My Arm Glassed Up," Weekend Telegraph (England), September 16, 1966.

149. "In a Radio Broadcast Beamed ... ," SR, 38 (November 26, 1955), 8-9.

149a. "In Awe of Words," Exonian, 224 (March 3, 1954), 4; rptd. in Nathaniel Benchley's Introduction to "JS" in Writers at Work: The Paris R Interviews, Fourth Series, ed. George Plimpton (New York: Viking Press, 1976), 182-83.

150. "The Inside," The Iron Gate of Jack and Charlie's "21." New York: The Jack Kriendler Memorial Foundation, 1950. p. 27. [In memory of John Carl Kriendler for the benefit of the New York Heart Association.]

151. Introduction to The World of Li'l Abner by Al Capp. New York: Farrar, Straus and Young, 1953.

152. "It Was Dark As Hell," They Were There: The Story of World War II and How It Came About, ed. C. Riess. New York: Putnam's, 1944. pp. 584-85.

153. "Jalopies I Cursed and Loved," Holiday, 16 (July 1954), 44-45; 89-90. Also in Ten Years of Holiday, eds. the Holiday editors. New York: Simon and Schuster, 1956. pp. 439-44.

154. "JS's Press Conference," Scene, 15 (December 27, 1962), 22 [Interview by Gordon Williams].

155. "The Joan in All of Us," SR, 39 (January 14, 1956), 17.

156. "JS: The Art of Fiction XLV," Paris R, 12 (Fall 1969), 161-88 [Interview].

157. "Let's Go After the Neglected: A Plea for Equal Effort on Treasure Beneath the Seas 'Inner Space' Exploration," Popular Science, 189 (September 1966), 84-87.

158. "The Light That Still Shines," Daily Express, July 17, 1943. p. 2.

159. " ... Like Captured Fireflies" (JS Says a Great Teacher Is One of the Great Artists), CTA Journal, 51 (November 1955), 6-8.

160. "Madison Avenue and the Election," SR, 39 (March 31, 1956), 11.

161. "The Mail I've Seen," SR, 39 (August 4, 1956), 16, 34.

162. "Making of a New Yorker," New York Times Magazine. February 1, 1953. VI, Pt. 3, p. 26; February 22, 1953. VI, 4. Also in The Empire City: A Treasury of New York, ed. Alexander Klein. New York: Rinehart, 1955. pp. 469-75.

163. "Man with a Ski Nose," This Was Your War, ed. Frank Brookhauser. New York: Dell, 1963.

164. "Miracle Island of Paris," Holiday, 19 (February 1956), 43.

165. "Mixed Battery--Can You See These Girls Going Back to the Old Jobs," Daily Express, July 8, 1943. p. 2.

166. "A Model T Named 'It,' " Ford Times, 45 (July 1953), 34-39.

> High Gear, ed. Evan Jones. New York: Bantam Books, 1955. pp. 64-66.

167. "More About Aristocracy: Why Not a World Peerage?" SR, 38 (December 10, 1955), 11.

168. "Mulligan Had a Lucky Comrade, " Daily Express, August 21, 1943. p. 2.

169. "Mulligan Knows What He Wants ... And Gets It, " Daily Express, August 14, 1943. p. 2.

170. "Mulligan Won't Take a Stripe, " Daily Express, August 7, 1943. p. 2.

171. "My Dear Friend Genya ..., " (a letter to a Russian friend) Reader's Digest, 89 (September 1966), 128 [Condensed from Newsday, July 11, 1966].

172. "My Short Novels, " Wings, 26 (October 1953), 1-8 (Literary Guild Review). Also in English Journal, 43 (March 1954), 147.

> [Excerpt from Wings]; SHC, pp. 38-40.

173. "My War with the Ospreys, " Holiday, 21 (March 1957), 72-73; 163-65. Also in Essays Today 3, ed. M. Ludwig. New York: Harcourt, Brace, 1958. Also in Reader's Digest, 70 (May 1957), 61-64 [Condensed from Holiday].

174. "Mystery of Life, " The Treasure Chest, ed. James Donald Adams. New York: Dutton, 1946. pp. 371-72.

> [From Sea of Cortez.]

175. "Noble John, " Daily Express, October 26, 1962.

> [Interview by Henry Lowrie.]

176. "Nobody Ever Gets Killed in a War, " Daily Express, October 7, 1943. p. 2.

177. "The Novel Might Benefit by the Discipline, the Terseness of the Drama," Stage, 15 (January 1938), 50-51.

178. "Of Beef and Men" (recipe), Famous Recipes by Famous People, ed. Herbert Cerivin. San Francisco: Lane, 1940.

179. "On Learning Writing," Writer's Yearbook, No. 34, 1963. Cincinnati: F. and W. Publishing, 1963. p. 10.

180. "One American in Paris (A Plea for Tourists)," Punch, 228 (January 26, 1955), 142-53.

181. "One American in Paris (Reality and Illusion)," Punch, 227 (November 17, 1954), 616-17.

182. "One American in Paris," Holiday in France, selected and decorated by L. Bemelmans. Boston: Houghton Mifflin, 1957. p. 141.

     [This consists of the four Holiday articles: "Miracle Island of Paris," "What Is the Real Paris?," "The Yank in Europe," and "Discontinuing the People of Paris," reprinted in that order as a single essay.]

183. "One More for Lady Luck," Star Reporters and 34 of Their Stories, ed. Ward Greene. New York: Random House, 1948. pp. 320-24.

184. "Our Rigged Morality," Coronet, 47 (March 1960), 144-47. Also in Fabulous Yesterdays, ed. Lewis W. Gellenson. New York: Harper, 1961.

     [S. and Adlai Stevenson, an exchange of letters.]

185. "Over There," Ladies' Home Journal, 61 (February 1944), 20-21. Also in The Ladies' Home Treasury, eds. John Mason Brown and the editors of The Ladies' Home Journal. New York: Simon & Schuster, 1956. ["The Ground Crew" in Once There Was a War, pp. 36-39.]

186. "A Plea for Tourists," Punch, 228 (January 26, 1955), 148-49.

187. "A Plea to Teachers," NEA Journal, 44 (September 1955), 359. Also in SR, 38 (April 30, 1955), 24.

188. "Poker for Keeps," Masterpieces of War Reporting, ed. Louis L. Snyder. New York: Julius Messner, 1962. p. 314.

189. "Positano," Harper's Bazaar, [n. v.] (May 1953), 158, 185, 187, 188, 194.

    Harper's Bazaar, [n. v.] (August 1953), 41, 68, 70.

190. Positano, Salerno: Eute provinciale per il Turismo, 1954 [First English-language separate edition].

191. "Preface to the Compass Edition" in Story Writing by Edith Ronald Mirrielees. New York: Viking Press, 1962.

192. "A President ..., Not a Candidate," Washington, D. C.: Democratic Convention Program Book Committee, 1964.

193. "A Primer on the 30s," Esquire, 103 (June 1960), 85-93.

194. "Prologue: I Go Back to Ireland," Collier's, 131 (January 31, 1953), 48-50.

195. "Ragged Crew," True, 44 (February 1963), 33-35; 79-82.

196. "Random Thoughts on Random Dogs," Cold Noses and Warm Hearts, ed. Corey Ford. Englewood Cliffs, N. J.: Prentice-Hall, 1958. p. 1.

    SR, 38 (October 8, 1955), 11. Also in SR Treasury, ed. SR. New York: Simon and Schuster, 1957. pp. 529-31.

197. "Rationale," SHC. pp. 308-309.

198. "Reality and Illusion," Punch, 227 (November 17, 1954), 616-17 (See 181).

199. "Report on America," Punch, 228 (June 22, 1955), 754-55.

200.   "Robert Capa: An Appreciation by J.S.," Images of
       War by Robert Capa.   New York: Grossman, 1964.
       p. 7.

       [This is a special edition assembled by his bro-
       ther Cornell, also a photographer] [Introduction to
       the book].

201.   "Robert Capa," Photography, 35 (September 1954), 48-
       53.

202.   "The Routing at a Bomber Station," This Was Your
       War, ed. Frank Brookhauser.   New York: Dell,
       1963.

203.   "The Secret Weapon We Were Afraid to Use," Collier's,
       131 (January 10, 1953), 9-13.

204.   Selected Essays of J.S., eds.   Hidekazu Hirose and
       Kiyoshi Nakayama.   Tokyo: Shinozake Shorin Press,
       1981.

       Including the following essays: "Autobiography:
       Making of a New Yorker"; "A Primer on the 30s";
       "Jalopies I Cursed and Loved"; "How to Tell Good
       Guys from Bad Guys"; "My War with the Ospreys";
       "Conversation at Sag Harbor"; "I Go Back to Ire-
       land."

205.   "Session with S.," Daily Express, June 15, 1957.   p.
       7.

       [Interview by Eve Perrick.]

206.   "Some Random and Randy Thoughts on Books," The
       Author Looks at Format, ed. Ray Freiman.   New
       York: The American Institute of Graphic Arts,
       1951.   pp. 27-34.

207.   "Some Thoughts on Juvenile Delinquency," SR, 38 (May
       28, 1955), 22.

208.   "Song of the Disgusted Modern," Monterey Beacon, 1
       (February 1, 1935), 7.

209.   "The Soul and Guts of France," Collier's, 130 (August
       30, 1952), 26ff.

210. "The Spivacks Beat the Odds": Condensed from The Journal of American Medical Association in Reader's Digest, 73 (October 1958), 153-54. See "Dedication."

211. "The Stars Point to Shafter," Progressive Weekly, December 24, 1938 [n. p.].

212. "S. in Vietnam," Daily Sketch, January 6, 1967. p. 6.

213. "S's Critics--Natural Enemies," Sunday Times, September 24, 1961. p. 15.

[Interview by Atticus].

214. "S's New Mood: I Am Scared, Boastful But Also Humble," Daily Express, January 15, 1965 [n. p.].

[Interview by Herbert Kretzmer].

215. "S's Voices of America," Scholastic, 65 (November 3, 1954), 15f.

216. "The Stevenson Spirit," The Faces of Five Decades, selected from Fifty Years of the New Republic, 1914-1964. Introduced by A. M. Schlesinger, Jr. New York: Simon and Schuster, 1964. p. 322.

217. "The Summer Before," Punch, 228 (May 25, 1955), 647-51.

218. "A Teddy Bear Called Miz Hicks," News Chronicle, January 18, 1960 [n. p.].

219. "Then My Arm Glassed Up," Weekend Telegraph, 103 (September 16, 1966), 46. Also in Sports Illustrated, 23 (December 20, 1965), [n. p.].

220. "They Don't Talk About Anything Else When Bob Hope's Coming," Daily Express, July 31, 1943. p. 2.

221. "A Thing Is Bigger Than a Scramble," Daily Express, July 23, 1943. p. 2.

222. "Tommy Gets Well," Daily Express, January 30, 1943. p. 2.

223. "Trade Wind: Predictions of Reviews East of Eden Would Receive," SR, 37 (February 27, 1954), 8.

224. "Troopship: Condensed from New York Herald Tribune," Reader's Digest, 44 (March 1944), 67-70.

225. "Trust Your Luck," SR, 40 (January 12, 1957), 42-44.

226. "Trust Your Luck," From Paragraph to Essay Readings for Progress in Writing by Woodrow Ohlson and Frank L. Hammond. New York: Scribner's, 1963. pp. 192-96.

227. "The Vegetable War," SR, 39 (July 21, 1956), 34-35.

228. "What Is the Real Paris?" Holiday, 18 (December 1955), 94.

229. "What Sort of Letter Do You Write to Your Soldier?" Daily Express, August 6, 1943. p. 2.

230. "Who Said the Old Lady Was Dying?" (Article on London theatre). Evening Standard (England), August 1, 1952 [n. p.].

231. "Women and Children in the U. S. S. R.," Ladies' Home Journal, 65 (February 1948), 44-59.

232. "The Women Watch Their Men," The Treasure Chest, ed. J. Donald Adams. New York: Dutton, 1946. pp. 374-75.

233. "The Wrath Hasn't Left S.," Daily Mail, September 18, 1961. p. 8.

    [Interview by Kenneth Allsop.]

234. "Writer's Mail," The Pick of Punch, ed. Nicholas Bentley. Foreword by Malcolm Muggeridge. London: Andre Deutsch, 1956.

    Punch, 229 (November 2, 1955), 512-13.

235. "The Yank in Europe," Holiday, 19 (January 1956), 25.

236. "You Don't Have to Be Angry to Write Good Books,"

Daily Express, December 13, 1962.

[Interview by Peter Grosvenor.]

237. "Your Audiences Are Wonderful," Sunday Times, August 10, 1952. p. 5.

G. PUBLISHED LETTERS, JOURNALS, AND DIARIES

238. "The Americans Embark for War," PS (1943). pp. 575-78.

239. "Appendix," The Acts of King Arthur and His Noble Knights, ed. Chase Horton. New York: Farrar, Straus and Giroux, 1976, pp. 296-394.

[72 letters to Elizabeth Otis and Chase Horton.]

240. "Battle Scene," PS (1943). p. 585-88.

241. Braley, Berton. "A Letter of J. S.," Morgan Sails the Caribbean. New York: Macmillan, 1934. pp. vii-viii.

[S. gives his permission to the author to use certain incidents from Cup of Gold.]

242. "A Day, a Mood, a Faith," Good Housekeeping, [n. v.] (December 1967), 82-83.

243. "No entry."

244. The First Watch. Los Angeles: Ward Ritchie Press, 1947. S's humorous letter of thanks for the gift of a watch. 6 pp.

[Limited to 60 copies; 10 for the use of the author and 50 copies for presentation by Marguerite and Louis Henry Cohn.]

245. "No entry."

246. "Izvestia published S letter apologizing to Soviet writers who were his hosts during 1963 visit for mixup over copies of his 1962 Nobel Prize speech and mimeo-

graphing thank-you notes he sent to them and acci-
dentally to others he had never met, " New York
Times, August 30, 1964. p. 24.

247. JS--A Letter Written in Reply to a Request for a Statement about His Ancestry, together with the letter
originally submitted by the Friends of Democracy.
Stamford, Conn. : Overbrook Press, 1940. 13 pp.
[350 copies].

248. JS Replies. New York: Friends of Democracy, 1940.
A letter written in reply to a request for a statement about his ancestry, together with the letter
originally submitted by the Friends of Democracy.
A printed leaflet containing an exchange of letters
between the author and the Rev. L. M. Birkhead,
national director of the Friends of Democracy.
Stamford, Conn. : The Overbrook Press, 1940. 2
pp. [350 copies only].

249. Journal of a Novel: The "East of Eden" Letters. New
York: Viking Press, 1969.

250. A Letter from JS [n. p.]. Roxburghe and Zamorano
Clubs, 1964 [S's letter to Professor Carruth]. 6
pp. [150 copies printed by Sherwood and Katharine
Grover].

251. "A Letter from S, " The Thinking Dog's Man by Ted
Patrick. New York: Random House, 1964.

Contains S's letter explaining why he could not
write an introduction for this book.

252. Letter from S on page following title, as well as dust
jacket, of Greek edition of East of Eden and re-
produced in the catalog of An Exhibition of American
and Foreign Editions. Austin, Texas: Humanities
Research Center, University of Texas, 1963. p.
27.

253. Letter from S to Jacqueline Kennedy after the assassi-
nation of President Kennedy is quoted in The Death
of a President by William Manchester. New York:
Harper & Row, 1967. p. 563.

254. "A Letter on Criticism, " Colorado Q, 4 (Autumn 1955),
218-19. Also in SHC. pp. 52-53.

255. "A Letter to Inmates of the Connecticut State Prison," Monthly Record, a monthly journal devoted to the interests of the inmates [n. v.] (June, 1938), [n. p.].

256. Letters from JS. St. Louis, Missouri: National Student Committee for Victory in Vietnam, 1967.

256a. Letters from S to Mrs. Grover, April 12, 1966; in JS: His Language; Introduction by James D. Hart, California, 1970.

257. "Letters to Alicia," a series of letters addressed to Alicia (Patterson Guggenheim), published in Newsday, starting November 20, 1965. Alicia is the wife of the editor and publisher of Newsday. [Also in Sunday Bulletin, News and Views Section, Philadelphia.]

258. Letters to Elizabeth, eds. Florian Shasky, and Susan Riggs. Introduction by Carlton Sheffield. San Francisco: Book Club of California, 1978.

259. "No entry. "

260. "More of Pvt. Big Train Mulligan, " PS (1943). pp. 582-85.

261. "Postscript from S, " SHC. pp. 307-08.

262. "Pvt. Big Train Mulligan, " PS (1943). pp. 578-82.

263. "No entry. "

264. "No entry. "

265. S. : A Life in Letters, eds. Elaine Steinbeck and Robert Wallsten. New York: Viking Press, 1975.

266. "S's Suggestion for an Interview with Joseph Henry Jackson, " Lisca (ed.), pp. 859-62.

267. "The Way It Seems to JS, " Occident [n. v.] (Fall 1936), [n. p.].

268. "Why Soldiers Won't Talk, " PS (1943). pp. 588-90.

269. "No entry. "

H. PUBLISHED SPEECHES

270. His Nobel Prize Acceptance Speech on December 10, 1962, quoted in Contemporary Authors, 2. Michigan: Gale Research, 1963. p. 184.

271. "His Nobel Prize Acceptance Speech," Story, Issue 2, 36 (March-April 1963). New York: Story Magazine, 1962.

272. "JS's Acceptance Speech for the Nobel Prize for Literature in 1962," Vogue, 141 (March 1, 1963), 16. Also in Donohue (ed.), pp. 293-95.

273. "JS's (Nobel Prize) Acceptance Speech," Vogue, 141 (March 1, 1963), 16.

274. "Man's Hope: S in Stockholm; Excerpt from His Address," Newsweek, 60 (December 24, 1962), 67.

275. "Nobel Prize Acceptance Speech and the Presentation by Anders Osterling," Nobel Prize Lectures (1901-1967), ed. Horst Frentz. New York: American Elsevier Publishing Co., 1969. pp. 575-77.

276. "Nobel Prize Acceptance Speech," A Supplement to the Book-of-the-Month-Club News. New York: Book-of-the-Month Club, 1962 [4 pp.].

277. O. Henry's Full House (1952). [Copyrighted in 1952 by 20th Century-Fox Film Corporation, consisting of five O. Henry stories. Narrated by J. S.]

278. "Speech Accepting the Nobel Prize for Literature, Stockholm, December 10, 1962." New York: Viking Press, 1962 [3,200 copies printed].

279. "To the Swedish Academy; Nobel Prize Acceptance Speech," Story, 139 (1963), 6-8.

I. COLLECTED WORKS

280. The Portable S., ed. with an introduction by Pascal Covici, Jr. New York: Viking Press, 1971 (1943, 1946 eds.).

[Excerpts from The Long Valley, The Pastures
of Heaven, Tortilla Flat, In Dubious Battle, The
Grapes of Wrath, Sea of Cortez, "About Ed Ricketts," Cannery Row, and East of Eden; the complete
novels, Of Mice and Men, The Red Pony; excerpts
also from Travels with Charley; two uncollected
stories--"The Affair at 7, rue de M--" and "How
Mr. Hogan Robbed a Bank," plus Steinbeck's "Nobel
Prize Acceptance Speech."]

281. The Short Novels of J. S.   Introduction by Joseph Henry Jackson. New York: Viking Press, 1953.

[Tortilla Flat, The Red Pony, Of Mice and Men,
The Moon Is Down, Cannery Row, and The Pearl.]

282. The S. Omnibus, ed. Pascal Covici. London: Heinemann, 1950.

[Excerpts from The Long Valley, The Pastures
of Heaven, Tortilla Flat, In Dubious Battle, The
Grapes of Wrath, Sea of Cortez, The Moon Is Down,
and Bombs Away; complete texts of Of Mice and
Men and The Red Pony.]

J.   REFERENCES TO UNPUBLISHED MANUSCRIPTS
AND LETTERS

N. B.: For unpublished manuscripts and
letters, consult such outstanding Steinbeck
bibliographies and catalogues as those by
Goldstone-Payne (1974), Gross-Hayman
(1979), Bradford Morrow Bookseller (1980),
and Riggs (1980). See also A Handbook for
Steinbeck Collectors, Librarians, and Scholars (SMS, No. 11), ed. T. Hayashi, 1981.

PART TWO: WORKS ABOUT JOHN STEINBECK

A. BIBLIOGRAPHIES

283. Beyer, Preston. "The Joad Newsletter," SQ, 4 (Fall 1971), 105-06.

284. _____. "JS: The Forming of a Collection," SQ, 12 (Winter-Spring 1979), 32-42; reprinted in A Handbook for S. Collectors, Librarians, and Scholars (SMS, No. 11) ed. T. Hayashi, 1981. pp. 9-18.

285. _____. "Memorial Statement in Honor of Adrian H. Goldstone," SQ, 12 (Winter-Spring 1979), 29-31; reprinted in A Handbook for S Collectors, Librarians, and Scholars (SMS, No. 11), ed. T. Hayashi, 1981. pp. 1-3.

286. _____, and Donald L. Siefker. "JS--Brief Mention," SQ, 6 (Summer 1973), 90-92.

287. _____, and _____. "JS: Brief Mention," SQ, 7 (Spring 1974), 57-59.

288. Bradford Morrow Bookseller, Ltd. see Morrow, Bradford.

289. Cox, Martha Heasley. "The S. Collection in the S. Research Center, San Jose University," SQ, 11 (Summer-Fall 1978), 96-99; reprinted in A Handbook for S Collectors, Librarians, and Scholars (SMS, No. 11), ed. T. Hayashi, 1981. pp. 29-32.

290. Davis, Robert Con. "Selected Bibliography," in his 20th Century Interpretations of "The G of W," 1982. pp. 154-57.

291. Davis, Robert Murray. "Selected Bibliography," in his S: A Collection of Critical Essays, Englewood Cliffs, N.J.: Prentice-Hall, 1972. pp. 181-83.

292. DeMott, Robert. S's Reading: A Catalogue of Books Owned and Borrowed. New York: Garland, 1983?

293. _____. "An Unnoticed S Item," SQ, 5 (Summer-Fall 1972), 117.

294. Dunbar, Maurice. "Adrian Homer Goldstone, Bibliophile (1897-1977)," SQ, 11 (Winter 1978), 4-5; reprinted in A Handbook for S Collectors, Librarians, and Scholars (SMS, No. 11), ed. T. Hayashi, 1981. pp. 4-5.

294a. Gerbereux, Robert Louis. "The JS Room at the Southampton College Library," SQ, 13 (Summer-Fall 1980), 69-71.

295. Goldstone, Adrian H. "Book Collecting and S," SJS, 1 (November 1975), 129-35.

296. _____, and John R. Payne. JS: A Bibliographical Catalogue of the Adrian H. Goldstone Collection. Austin: University of Texas Humanities Research Center, 1974.

297. Gross, John, and Lee Richard Hayman (eds). JS: A Guide to the Collection of the Salinas Public Library. Salinas, Cal.: Salinas Public Library, 1979.

298. Harmon, Robert B. The First Editions of JS. Los Altos, Cal.: Hermes, 1978 [pamphlet].

299. _____. JS: Toward a Bibliography of Bibliographies. San Jose, Cal.: Dibco Press, 1973 [8 pp.].

300. "No entry."

301. Hayashi, Tetsumaro. "A Guide to S Studies: Questions and Answers," A Study Guide to S (Part II), ed. T. Hayashi, 1979. pp. 7-18.

302. _____. A Handbook for S Collectors, Librarians, and Scholars (SMS, No. 11) (Muncie, Ind.: S Society, Ball State University, 1981).

303. _____. "JS: A Selected Bibliographical Checklist," S's Prophetic Vision of America, eds. T. Hayashi and K. D. Swan, 1976. pp. 102-07.

304. _____. A New S Bibliography (1929-1971). Metuchen, N. J.: Scarecrow Press, 1973.

305. _____. "Selected Bibliography: Books about S," S's Women (SMS, No. 9) ed. T. Hayashi, 1979. pp. 53-54.

306. _____. "A Selected Bibliography: S and the Arthurian Theme," S and the Arthurian Theme (SMS, No. 5), ed. T. Hayashi, 1975. pp. 44-46.

307. _____. "A Selected Bibliography," S's Literary Dimensions: A Guide to Comparative Studies, ed. T. Hayashi, 1973. pp. 174-79.

308. _____. "A Selected Checklist of Recent Books on JS Published in the United States," SQ, 13 (Winter-Spring 1980), 61-62.

309. _____. "A Selected Checklist of The Long Valley Criticism," A Study Guide to S's "The Long Valley," ed. T. Hayashi, 1976. pp. 133-36.

310. _____. "A Selected Guide to Library Resources in the United States for Visiting Scholars," A Handbook for Collectors, Librarians, and Scholars (SMS, No. 11), ed. T. Hayashi, 1981. pp. 41-46.

311. _____, and Donald L. Siefker (comps.). The Special S Collection of the Ball State University Library: A Bibliographical Handbook. Muncie, Ind.: Steinbeck Society, Ball State University, 1972.

312. _____, and Roy S. Simmonds. "JS's British Publications," SQ, 8 (Summer-Fall 1975), 79-89.

313. Hayman, Lee Richard. "Collecting S: The Endless Hunt," SQ, 12 (Winter-Spring 1979), 48-53; reprinted in A Handbook for S Collectors, Librarians,

and Scholars (SMS, No. 11), ed. T. Hayashi, 1981.
pp. 24-28.

314. Libman, Valentina A. (comp.). Russian Studies of
American Literature: A Bibliography, tr. Robert
V. Allen; ed. Clarence Gohdes. Chapel Hill: Uni-
versity of North Carolina Press, 1969.

315. Lisca, Peter. "Bibliography," JS, "The Grapes of
Wrath": Text and Criticism, ed. P. Lisca, 1972.
pp. 869-81.

316. Morrow, Bradford, and Harry Valentine (comps.). JS:
A Collection of Books and Manuscripts Formed by
Harry Valentine of Pacific Grove, CA. Introduction by John Payne. Santa Barbara, Cal.: Bradford Morrow, 1980 [Catalogue 8].

317. Payne, John R. "JS in the Humanities Research Center,
the University of Texas at Austin," SQ, 11 (Summer-
Fall 1978), 100-02; reprinted in A Handbook for S
Collectors, Librarians, and Scholars (SMS, No. 11),
ed. T. Hayashi, 1981. pp. 33-34.

318. Plummer, Linda. "The S Collection in the Salinas
Public Library, Salinas, California," SQ, 12 (Summer-Fall 1979), 122-23; reprinted in A Handbook
for S Collectors, Librarians, and Scholars (SMS,
No. 11), ed. T. Hayashi, 1981. pp. 35-36.

319. Riggs, Susan F. A Catalogue of the JS Collection at
Stanford University, with an introduction by Jack-
son J. Benson. Stanford, Cal.: Stanford University
Libraries, 1980.

320. _____, and Millicent Dillon. "Stanford's JS Collection," The Imprint of the Stanford Libraries Associates, 1 (April 1975), 6-15.

321. _____. "The S Collection in the Department of
Special Collections, Stanford University Libraries,"
SQ, 11 (Summer-Fall 1978), 102-03; reprinted in A
Handbook for S Collectors, Librarians, and Scholars
(SMS, No. 11), ed. T. Hayashi, 1981. p. 37.

322. Siefker, Donald L. "A Checklist of Journals and Reference Guides That Index the SQ and SMS," SQ, 14
(Summer-Fall 1981), 135.

323. _____. "Cumulative Index to the SQ, 1-10 (1968-1977)," SQ, 11 (Spring 1978), 37-61.

324. _____. "JS: Brief Mention." See Beyer, Preston. SQ, 7 (Spring 1974).

325. _____. "S and Bestsellers," SQ, 11 (Summer-Fall 1978), 106-07.

326. Simmonds, Roy S. "JS: Works Published in the British Magazine Argosy," SQ, 4 (Fall 1971), 101-05.

327. _____. "JS's World War II Dispatches: An Annotated Checklist," Serif, 11 (Summer 1974), 21-30.

328. _____. "The Typescripts of S's America and Americans," SQ, 4 (Fall 1971), 120-21.

329. Smith, Juanita. "The S Collection in Honor of Elizabeth R. Otis at the Alexander M. Bracken Library, Ball State University," SQ, 11 (Summer-Fall 1978), 103-05; reprinted in A Handbook for S Collectors, Librarians, and Scholars (SMS, No. 11) ed. T. Hayashi, 1981. pp. 38-40.

330. Woodress, James. "JS" in American Fiction, 1900-1950: A Guide to Information Sources. Detroit: Gale Research Co., 1974, pp. 183-93.

331. Yamashita, Mitsuaki. "A Survey of JS Bibliographies in Japan," Persica, 5 (January 1978), 93-122.

B. BIOGRAPHIES

N. B.: Professor Jackson J. Benson's authorized biography of S is soon to be published by the Viking Press.

332. Astro, Richard. "JS," Dictionary of Literary Biography. Detroit: Gale Research, 1981. IX: 43-68.

333. _____. "JS: A Biographical Portrait," JS: A Dictionary of His Fictional Characters, ed. T. Hayashi, 1976. pp. 1-24.

334. _____. "JS: Prospectus for a Literary Biography,"
     SQ, 4 (Summer 1971), 76-80.

334a. Benchley, Nathaniel. Introduction to "JS," in Writings
     at Work: The Paris R Interviews, Fourth Series,
     ed. George Plimpton (New York: Viking Press,
     1976), pp. 182-84.

335. Benson, Frederick R. "S," McGraw-Hill Encyclopedia
     of World Biography. New York: McGraw-Hill,
     1973. pp. 191-93.

336. Benson, Jackson J. " 'To Tom, Who Lived It': JS
     and the Man from Weedpatch," JML, 5 (April 1976),
     151-94.

337. Covici, Pascal, Jr. "Biographical and Bibliographical
     Portrait," in The Viking Portable S, ed. Covici,
     1971. pp. xxi-xlii.

338. Covington, Deborah B. The Argus Book Shop: A
     Memoir. West Cornwall, Conn.: Tarrydiddle
     Press, 1977 ["Experiences with S," pp. 108-14].

339. Cox, Martha Heasley. "In Search of JS: His People
     and His Land," SJS, 1 (November 1975), 41-60.

339a. _____. "S's Family Portraits: The Hamiltons,"
     SQ, 14 (Winter-Spring 1981), 23-32 [With Hamilton
     family photo].

340. Crouch, Steve. S Country. Palo Alto, Cal.: Ameri-
     can West Publishing Co., 1973.

341. Fensch, Thomas. S and Covici: The Story of a Friend-
     ship. Middlebury, Vt.: Ericksson, 1979.

342. Fisher, Shirley. "S's Days in Sag Harbor," New York
     Times, Sunday, December 3, 1978. LI: 20.

343. French, Warren. "JS," Academic American Encyclo-
     pedia. Princeton, N.J.: Areté Publishing Co.,
     1981. [n. p.].

343a. _____. "JS," in "American Novelists, 1910-1945,"
     Dictionary of Literary Biography. Detroit: Gale
     Research, 1981. IX, 247-71.

344. Hedgpeth, Joel W. Philosophy on Cannery Row," in S: The Man and His Work, eds. Astro and Hayashi, 1971. pp. 89-129.

345. _____. The Outer Shores: Part I. Ed Ricketts and JS Explore the Pacific Coast. Eureka, Cal.: Mad River Press, 1978.

346. _____. The Outer Shores: Part II. Breaking Through. Eureka, Cal.: Mad River Press, 1979.

347. Kiernan, Thomas. The Intricate Music: A Biography of JS. Boston: Little, Brown, 1979.

348. Otis, Elizabeth R. "Autobiography," SQ, 15 (Winter-Spring 1982), 9-10.

349. Powell, Lawrence Clark. California Classics. Los Angeles: Ward Ritchie Press, 1971. pp. 220-30.

350. Preston, Dickson. "O Fair Rocinante Who Has Seen the World: Welcome: JS's Faithful Companion Now Is a Resident of the Eastern Shore," Sun Magazine, Feb. 20, 1972. pp. 14, 16.

351. Riggs, Susan F. "S at Stanford," Stanford Magazine, 4 (Fall-Winter 1976), 14-21.

352. Schmitz, Anne-Marie. In Search of S. Los Altos, Cal.: Hermes Publications, 1978 [An Account of S's Homes; Richard Mayer, a photographer].

353. Sheffield, Carlton A. "College Pal Recalls: S Doubted His Talents," Mercury (San Jose, Cal.), December 6, 1974. p. 83.

354. _____. "Letters to a Friend Indicate S Doubted His Talent," Palo Alto Times, Nov. 14, 1974. p. 3.

355. Spies, George H., III. "Van Wyck Brooks on JS: A Reminiscence," SQ, 4 (Fall 1971), 106-07.

356. Street, Webster. "Remembering JS," SJS, 1 (November 1979), 108-27 [Interview by Martha Heasley Cox].

357. _____. "JS: A Reminiscence," in S: The Man and His Work, eds. Astro and Hayashi, 1971. pp. 35-41.

358. Thesling, William B. "JS," Dictionary of Literary
        Biography. VII, pt. 2, pp. 271-76.

359. Valjean, Nelson. JS: The Errant Knight: An Intimate
        Biography of His California Years. San Francisco
        Chronicle Books, 1975.

C. SURVEYS (ESSAYS) OF STEINBECK CRITICISM

360. Astro, Richard. "Advice to a Graduate Student," SQ,
        6 (Spring 1973), 45-46.

360a. Buerger, Daniel. " 'History' and Fiction in East of
        Eden Criticism," SQ, 14 (Winter-Spring 1981), 6-14.

361. Cox, Martha. "Advice to a Student of S," SQ, 6
        (Spring 1973), 47-48.

361a. DeMott, Robert. "Looking East from California's Shore:
        S in Japan," SJS, 6 (February 1980), 54-58.

362. _____. "New Directions in S Studies," SQ, 10 (Sum-
        mer-Fall 1977), 69-70.

363. _____. "S Criticism: A Retrospect," SQ, 6 (Spring
        1973), 42-44 [Joseph Fontenrose].

364. Ditsky, John. "Plenty of Room on The Wayward Bus,"
        SQ, 6 (Spring 1973), 48-49.

365. French, Warren. "How to Study S's Work Effectively,"
        SQ, 6 (Spring 1973), 50-51.

366. _____. "JS," Sixteen Modern American Authors, ed.
        Jackson R. Bryer, 1974. pp. 499-527.

367. Garcia, Reloy. "A Finer Filter and a Bigger Pan:
        Directions in S Criticism," SQ, 6 (Spring 1973),
        51-52.

367a. Hayashi, Tetsumaro. "A Brief Survey of S Criticism
        in the United States," Kyushu American Literature,
        14 (September 1972), 43-49.

368. _____ (ed.). JS: A Guide to the Doctoral Disserta-

tions (SMS, No. 1), Muncie, Ind.: S Society, Ball State University, 1971.

369. _____. "Recent S Studies in the United States: 1973-1975," Contemporary Communications, 2 (September 1974), 40-45.

370. "No entry."

371. Hayashi, Tetsumaro. "Recent S Studies in the United States," SQ, 4 (Summer 1971), 73-76; revised in S and the Sea, eds. R. Astro and J. W. Hedgpeth, 1975. pp. 11-13.

372. _____ (ed.). S and Hemingway: Dissertation Abstracts and Research Opportunities. Metuchen, N. J.: Scarecrow Press, 1980.

373. _____ (ed.). S Criticism: A Review of Book-Length Studies (1939-1973) (SMS, No. 4). Muncie, Ind.: S Society, 1974.

374. _____. "S Scholarship: Recent Trends in the United States," S's Literary Dimension: A Guide to Comparative Studies, ed. T. Hayashi, 1973. pp. 168-73.

375. Hirose, Hidekazu. "Japanese S Criticism in 1971; 1972-73; 1974-75," SQ, 1 (Fall 1973), 99-104; 8 (Spring 1975), 56-59; 10 (Spring 1977), 44-48. See Nakayama, Kiyoshi.

376. Lisca, Peter. "Editor's Introduction: The Pattern of Criticism," JS: "The Grapes of Wrath": Text and Criticism, ed. P. Lisca, 1972. pp. 695-707.

377. _____. "New Perspectives in S Studies," University of Windsor R, 8 (Spring 1973), 6-10.

378. _____. "A Survey of S Criticism, to 1971," S's Literary Dimension: A Guide to Comparative Studies, ed. T. Hayashi, 1973. pp. 148-67.

379. McDaniel, Barbara A. "JS: Recent Publications," West Coast R, 12 (January 1978), 55-59.

380. Nakayama, Kiyoshi. "S Criticism in Japan," SQ, 12

(Summer-Fall 1979), 115-22; 14 (Summer-Fall 1981),
105-11. See Hirose, Hidekazu (1971-77).

380a. Peterson, Richard F. "Research Opportunities in JS, "
S. and Hemingway: Dissertation Abstracts and Research Opportunities, ed. T. Hayashi, 1980. pp.
67-77.

381. Satyanarayana, M. R. "S Criticism in India: 1968-78, "
SQ, 14 (Winter-Spring 1981), 52-56.

381a. Sugiyama, Takahiko. "S Criticism: Present and Fu-
ture, " JS: East and West (SMS, No. 8), eds. T.
Hayashi, et al., 1978. pp. 1-6.

D. BOOKS ON JS INCLUDING COLLECTIONS OF
ESSAYS ON JS

N. B.: Consult the latest edition of Subject Guide to Books in Print and Cumulative Book Index.

382. Astro, Richard. JS and Edward F. Ricketts: The
Shaping of a Novelist. Minneapolis: University of
Minnesota Press, 1973.

383. _____, and Tetsumaro Hayashi (eds.). S: The Man
and His Work. Corvallis: Oregon State University
Press, 1971.

384. Davis, Robert Con (ed.). Twentieth Century Interpre-
tations: "The Grapes of Wrath": A Collection of
Critical Essays. Englewood Cliffs, N. J.: Prentice-
Hall, 1982.

385. Davis, Robert Murray (ed.). S: A Collection of Critical Essays. Englewood Cliffs, N. J.: Prentice-
Hall, 1972.

386. French, Warren. A Filmguide to "The Grapes of
Wrath. " Bloomington: Indiana University Press,
1973.

387. _____. JS. Rev. ed. Boston: Twayne, 1975.

388. Hayashi, Tetsumaro. JS: A Dictionary of His Fictional Characters. Metuchen, N. J.: Scarecrow Press, 1976.

389. _____ (ed.). S's Literary Dimension: A Guide to Comparative Studies. Metuchen, N. J.: Scarecrow Press, 1973.

390. _____ (ed.). A Study Guide to S: A Handbook to His Major Works ed. Metuchen, N. J.: Scarecrow Press, 1974.

391. _____ (ed.). A Study Guide to S (Part II). Metuchen, N. J.: Scarecrow Press, 1979.

392. _____ (ed.). A Study Guide to S's "The Long Valley," Ann Arbor, Mich.: Pierian Press, 1976.

393. _____, and Kenneth D. Swan (eds.). S's Prophetic Vision of America: Proceedings of the Bicentennial S Seminar Held on May 1, 1976 at Taylor University. Muncie, Ind.: S Society, 1976.

394. Hedgpeth, Joel W. (ed.). The Outer Shores: Part I: Ed Ricketts and JS Explore the Pacific Coast. Eureka, Cal.: Mad River Press, 1978.

395. _____ (ed.). The Outer Shores: Part II: Breaking Through. Eureka, Cal.: Mad River Press, 1978.

396. Jain, Sunita. S's Concept of Man: A Critical Study of His Novels. New Delhi, India: New Statesman Publishing Co., 1979.

397. Knox, Maxine, and Mary Rodriguez. S's Street: Cannery Row, San Raphael, Cal.: Presidio Press, 1980.

398. Levant, Howard. The Novels of JS: A Critical Study. Introduction by Warren French. Columbia: University of Missouri Press, 1974.

399. Lisca, Peter (ed.). "The Grapes of Wrath": Text and Criticism. New York: Viking Press, 1972.

400. _____. JS: Nature and Myth. New York: Crowell, 1978.

400a. _____. The Wide World of JS. New Brunswick,
N. J.: Rutgers University, 1958; reprinted in Staten
Island, N. Y.: Gordian Press, 1981.

401. McCarthy, Paul. JS (Modern Literary Monograph
Series). New York: Ungar, 1980.

402. Prabhakar, S. S. JS: A Study of Motifs of Dream and
Disillusionment. Hyderabad, India: Academic Publishers, 1976.

403. Rao, B. Bamachandra. The American Fictional Hero:
An Analysis of the Works of Fitzgerald, Wolfe, Far-
rell, Dos Passos, and S. Chaudigarh: Bahri, 1979;
New York: Asia Publishing House, 1979.

404. Satyanarayana, M. R. JS: A Study in the Theme of
Compassion. Hyderabad, India: Osmania University,
1977.

405. Schmitz, Anne-Marie. In Search of S (Photography by
Richard S. Mayer). Los Altos, Cal.: Hermes
Publications, 1978.

406. Shimomura, Noboru. A Study of JS: Mysticism in His
Novels. Tokyo, Japan: Hokuseido Press, 1982.

407. Sreenivasan, K. JS: A Study of His Novels. Trivan-
drum, India: College Book House, 1980.

408. Watt, F. S. New York: Grove Press, 1962; New
York: Chips, 1978.

409. Weber, Tom. All the Heroes Are Dead: The Ecology
of JS's "Cannery Row." San Francisco: Ramparts
Press, 1974.

410. Yano, Shigeharu. The Current of S's World. Tokyo:
Seibido Press, 1978-82 [I and II: 1978; III: 1979;
IV: 1982].

E. BOOKLETS, PAMPHLETS, ETC.

N. B.: Consult the latest edition of Subject Guide to Books in Print and Cumulative Book Index.

411. Astro, Richard. Edward F. Ricketts (Boise State University Western Writers Series, No. 21). Boise: Idaho State University, 1976.

412. _____, and Joel W. Hedgpeth (eds.). S of the Sea. Corvallis: Oregon State University, Sea Grant College Program, 1975.

413. Bennett, Robert. The Wrath of JS (1939). Darby, Pa.: Folcroft, 1973.

414. Carey, Gary K. "The Grapes of Wrath" Notes. Lincoln, Neb.: Cliffs Notes, 1981.

415. _____. "Of Mice and Men" Notes. Lincoln, Neb.: Cliffs Notes, 1981.

416. _____. "The Red Pony," "Chrysanthemums," "Flight" Notes. Lincoln, Neb.: Cliffs Notes, 1981.

417. Fitzwater, Eva. "The Pearl" Notes. Lincoln, Neb.: Cliffs Notes, 1981.

418. Fontenrose, Joseph. S's Unhappy Valley: A Study of "The Pastures of Heaven." Privately published by the author. 823 San Luis Road, Berkeley, Cal. 94707.

419. Gale, Robert L. Barron's Simplified Approach to S's "The Grapes of Wrath." Woodbury, N.Y.: Barron, 1981.

420. Gannett, Lewis. JS (1939). New York: Haskell, 1979.

421. Gray, James. JS (Pamphlets on American Writers Series, No. 94). Minneapolis: University of Minnesota Press, 1971.

422. Messner, Mike. Steinbeck Country in Dubious Homage. Salinas, Cal.: Privately published by author, 1979.

F. STEINBECK MONOGRAPH SERIES (1971-1981)

N. B.: SMS, Nos. 1-11 (1971-1981), ed. T. Hayashi. Muncie, Ind.: S Society, Ball State University, 1971-1981.

SMS, Nos. 1-11, 1971-1981, are annual
publications. After 1982, SMS will be published occasionally, when the funds are available.

423. SMS, No. 1, 1971. JS: A Guide to Doctoral Dissertations: A Collection of Dissertation Abstracts
(1946-1969), ed. T. Hayashi [See S. and Hemingway: Dissertation Abstracts and Research Opportunities, ed. T. Hayashi. Metuchen, N.J.: Scarecrow Press, 1980.]

424. SMS, No. 2, 1972. JS and D. H. Lawrence: Fictive
Voices and the Ethical Imperative by Reloy Garcia.

425. SMS, No. 3, 1973. JS as Fabulist by Lawrence William Jones; ed. Marston LaFrance.

426. SMS, No. 4, 1974. S Criticism: A Review of Book-
Length Studies (1939-1973), ed. T. Hayashi.

427. SMS, No. 5, 1975. S and the Arthurian Theme, ed.
T. Hayashi.

428. SMS, No. 6, 1976. S's Literary Achievement by Roy
S. Simmonds.

429. SMS, No. 7, 1977. Essays on "East of Eden" by John
Ditsky.

430. SMS, No. 8, 1978. JS: East and West, eds. T. Hayashi, Yasuo Hashiguchi, and Richard F. Peterson.

431. SMS, No. 9, 1979. S's Women: Essays in Criticism,
ed. T. Hayashi.

432. SMS, No. 10, 1980. S's Travel Literature: Essays
in Criticism, ed. T. Hayashi.

433. SMS, No. 11, 1981. A Handbook for S. Collectors,
Librarians, and Scholars, ed. T. Hayashi.

434. "No entry."

G. PROCEEDINGS OF S CONFERENCES

435. S Conference, Oregon State University, Corvallis, Oregon; directed by Richard Astro, 1970.
See S: The Man and His Work, eds. R. Astro and T. Hayashi. Corvallis: Oregon State University Press, 1971.

436. S Conference and Film Festival, San Jose State University, San Jose, CA; directed by Martha Heasley Cox, 1971.
See SQ, 4 (Summer 1971), eds. T. Hayashi, R. Astro, and M. H. Cox.

437. MLA S Society Meeting (I), New York City; directed by Daryl B. Adrian, 1972.
See the University of Windsor R, ed. John Ditsky, 8 (Spring 1973). [Conference topic: "Aspects of JS' Thought and Writings."]

438. MLA Steinbeck Society Meeting (II), Chicago; directed by T. Hayashi, 1973.
See SQ, 7 (Summer-Fall 1974). [Conference topic: "S: Comparative Studies."]

439. MLA S Society Meeting (III), New York; directed by Warren French, 1974.
See SQ, 9 (Winter 1976). [Conference topic: "JS and Naturalism."]

440. S and the Sea Conference, Oregon State University Marine Science Center, Newport, Oregon; directed by R. Astro and Joel W. Hedgpeth, 1974.
See S and the Sea, eds. R. Astro and J. W. Hedgpeth [Sea Grant Communications, Oregon State University, 1975].

441. MLA S Society Meeting (IV), San Francisco; directed by Martha Heasley Cox, 1975.
See SQ, 10 (Winter 1977) [Conference topic: "Environment as Meaning in JS's Work."]

442. Bicentennial S Conference, Taylor University, Upland, Indiana; directed by Kenneth D. Swan and T. Hayashi, 1976.
See S's Prophetic Vision of America, eds. T. Hayashi and K. D. Swan. Muncie, Ind.: S Society, 1976.

443. First International S Congress, Kyushu University, Fu-
      kuoka, Japan; directed by Yasuo Hashiguchi and T.
      Hayashi, 1976.
      See JS: East and West (SMS, No. 8), eds. T.
      Hayashi, Y. Hashiguchi, and Richard F. Peterson
      (S Society, 1978); Japanese translation by Shigeharu
      Yano. Tokyo, Japan: Hokuseido Press, 1982.

444. MLA S Society Meeting (V), New York; directed by
      Robert DeMott, 1976.
      See SQ, 10 (Summer-Fall 1977) [Conference top-
      ic: "New Directions in S Studies."]

445. MLA S Society Meeting (VI), Chicago; directed by
      Richard F. Peterson, 1977.
      See S's Women: Essays in Criticism (SMS, No.
      9), ed. T. Hayashi (S Society, 1979) [Conference
      topic: "S's Women."]

446. MLA S Society Meeting (VII), New York; directed by
      John Ditsky, 1978.
      See SQ, 12 (Summer-Fall 1979) [Conference top-
      ic: "Eden and After: JS's Later Works."

447. MLA S Society Meeting (VIII), San Francisco; directed
      by Robert DeMott, 1979.
      See SQ, 14 (Winter Spring 1981), ed. R. DeMott
      [Conference topic: "Mapping East of Eden."]

H. JOURNALS: SPECIAL STEINBECK ISSUES

448. The American Examiner: A Forum of Ideas, ed. Doug-
      las A. Noverr (Michigan State University American
      Studies Association), 6 (Fall-Winter 1978-79).

449. The Newsletter of the Steinbeck Society of Japan, ed.
      Shigeharu Yano. Tokyo: Reitaku University,
      1977-

450. San Jose Studies, eds. Martha Heasley Cox and Robert
      H. Woodward (San Jose University), 1 (November
      1975).

451. The Steinbeck Collector (1979-), ed. Robert B. Har-
      mon.

Bibliographic Research Library
964 Chapel Hill Way
San Jose, CA   95122

452.   The Steinbeck Quarterly, ed. Tetsumaro Hayashi (S Society, Ball State University, 1968-   ).

453.   The University of Windsor Review, ed. John Ditsky
(Canada), 8 (Spring 1973).

I.   DOCTORAL DISSERTATIONS (unpublished)

N. B.:   Consult DAI and S and Hemingway:
Dissertation Abstracts and Research Oppor-
tunities, ed. T. Hayashi.   Metuchen, N. J.:
Scarecrow Press, 1980.

454.   Anderson, Arthur Cummings.   "The Journey Motif in
the Fiction of JS: The Traveler Discovers Himself,"
Fordham University, 1976.   DAI, 37A (Nov-Dec
1970), 2867.

455.   Bose, Kumar.   "S: An Appraisal of His Thought and
Message," Bhagalpur University, India, 1977.

456.   Brown, Joyce Diann Compton.   "Animal Symbolism and
Imagery in JS's Fiction from 1929 through 1939,"
University of Southern Mississippi, 1972.   DAI, 33
(October 1972), 1716.

457.   Carr, Duane Ralph.   "JS: Twentieth-Century Romantic.
A Study of the Early Works," University of Tulsa,
1975.   DAI, 36A (March-April 1976), 6680.

458.   Davis, David Glenn.   "The Image of the Minister in
American Fiction," University of Tulsa, 1978.   DAI,
39A (July-August 1979), 882.

459.   Davis, Gary Corbett.   "JS in Films: An Analysis of
Realism in the Novel and in the Film--A Non-

Asterisk (*) indicates items later published as books.

teleological Approach, " University of Southern California, 1975. DAI, 36A (November-December 1975), 3170.

460. * Fensch, Thomas Charles. "Between Author and Editor: The Selected Correspondence of JS and Pascal Covici, 1945-1952, " Syracuse University, 1977. DAI, 38A (January-February 1978), 4427.

461. Fitzmaurice, James Earl. "Migration Epics of the Trans-Mississippi West, " University of Maryland, 1974. DAI, 35A (January-February 1975), 5399-400 [G of W].

462. Frost, Larry Don. "Behavioral Engineering in the American Novel, 1924-1972, " East Texas State University, 1978. DAI, 39A (November-December 1978), 3578 [G of W and East of Eden].

463. Gladstein, Mimi Reisel. "The Indestructible Woman in the Works of Faulkner, Hemingway, and S, " University of New Mexico, 1973. DAI, 35A (September-October 1974), 1655.

464. Govoni, Mark William. "Symbols for the Wordlessness: A Study of JS's East of Eden, " Ohio University, 1978. DAI, 39A (May 1979), 6701.

465. Griffith, Raymond L. "Dissonant Symphony: Multilevel Duality in the Fiction of JS, " Loyola University of Chicago, 1972. DAI, 33 (October 1972), 1723-24.

466. Hagy, Boyd Frederick. "A Study of the Changing Patterns of Melodrama as They Contributed to American Playwriting from 1920 to 1950, " Catholic University of America, 1978. DAI, 39A (September-October 1978), 1548-49 [Of Mice and Men].

467. Hughes, Robert S. "S's Short Stories: A Critical Study, " Indiana University at Bloomington, 1981.

468. * Jain, Sunita Goel. "JS's Concept of Man, " University of Nebraska, 1972. DAI, 33A (November-December 1972), 2937.

469. Kagan, Sheldon S. " 'Goin' Down the Road Feelin' Bad'--JS's The Grapes of Wrath and Migrant Folk-

lore, " University of Pennsylvania, 1971. <u>DAI</u>, 32A
(January-February 1972), 4507.

470. Koloc, Frederick Joseph. "JS's <u>In Dubious Battle</u>:
Backgrounds, Reputation, and Artistry. " <u>DAI</u>, 36A
(July-August 1975), 889.

471. Lewis, Clifford L. "JS: Architect of the Unconscious,"
University of Texas, Austin, 1972. <u>DAI</u>, 34A (July-
August 1973), 781.

472. McDaniel, Barbara Albrecht. "Self-Alienating Characters in the Fiction of JS, " North Texas State University, 1974. <u>DAI</u>, 35A (January-February 1975),
4534-35.

473. McTee, James David. "Underhill's Mystic Way and
the Initiation Theme in the Major Fiction of JS, "
East Texas State University, 1975. <u>DAI</u>, 36A
(March-April 1976), 6102.

474. Owens, Louis D. "A New Eye in the West: S's California Fiction, " University of California at Davis,
1981. <u>DAI</u>, 42A (March 1982), 4002.

475. Patterson, Angela. "The Women of JS's Novels in the
Light of Humanistic Psychology, " United States In-
ternational University, 1974. <u>DAI</u>, 35B (September-
October 1974), 1344.

476. Perez, Betty L. "The Collaborative Roles of JS and
Edward F. Ricketts in the Narrative Section of <u>Sea
of Cortez</u>, " University of Florida, Gainesville, 1972.
<u>DAI</u>, 34A (July-August 1973), 332.

477. "No entry. "

478. * Prabhakar, S. S. "A Study of Dream and Disillusionment in the Fiction of JS, " Andhra University, India,
1971.

479. Serota, Steve. "The Function of the Grotesque in the
Works of JS, " Oklahoma State University, 1973.
<u>DAI</u>, 35A (March-April 1975), 6733.

480. Spies, George Henry, III. "JS's <u>The Grapes of Wrath</u>
and Frederick Manfred's <u>The Golden Bowl</u>: A Com-

parative Study," Ball State University, 1973. <u>DAI</u>, 34A (November-December 1973), 3431-32.

481. * Sreenivasan, K. "The Novels of S: A Study of His Image of Man," University of Kerala, India, 1977.

482. Stuurmans, Harry. "JS's Lover's Quarrel with America," University of Michigan, 1973. <u>DAI</u>, 34A (January-February 1974), 5206.

483. Swan, Kenneth Dale. "Perspectives on the Fiction of JS: A Critical Review of Two Prominent S Critics --Peter Lisca and Warren French," Ball State University, 1974. <u>DAI</u>, 35A (September-October 1974), 1673.

484. TeMaat, Agatha. "JS: On the Nature of the Creative Process in the Early Years," University of Nebraska, Lincoln, 1975. <u>DAI</u>, 36A (January-February 1976), 5306.

485. Van DeVyvere, James. "Psychological Naturalism: The Jungian Myths of JS," University of Ottawa (Canada), 1979.

486. Winchell, Mark Royden. "One Foot in Paradise: The American Adam in the Modern World," Vanderbilt University, 1978. <u>DAI</u>, 39A (November-December 1978), 2935.

487. Wilson, Jerry W. "JS: Love, Work, and the Politics of Collectivity," University of Oklahoma, 1977. <u>DAI</u>, 39A (September 1979), 1578-79.

488. Winn, Harlan Harbour, III. "Short Story Cycles of Hemingway, S, Faulkner, and O'Connor," University of Oregon, 1975. <u>DAI</u>, 36A (January-February 1976), 4500.

489. Yancey, Anita V. R. "Winesburg, Ohio and The Pastures of Heaven: A Comparative Analysis of Two Studies on Isolation," Southern Mississippi University, 1972. <u>DAI</u>, 32 (1972), 5249A.

N. B.: DAI entries: Bound dissertations are available in most instances. Write to:

The University Microfilms
Xerox Corporation
300 N. Zeeb Road
Ann Arbor, Michigan 48106.

J. ARTICLES/ESSAYS IN JOURNALS, MAGAZINES,
     AND BOOKS

490. Abramson, Ben. Style. West Cornwall, Conn.: Deborah Benson Bookseller, 1977 [S/Faulkner/Hemingway/Cabell/Nathan/and Lawrence].

491. Alexander, Stanley. "Cannery Row: S's Pastoral Poem," WAL, 2 (1968), 281-95; reprinted in S: A Collection of Critical Essays, ed. R. M. Davis, 1972. pp. 135-48.

492. Asano, Toshio. "S's Sense for the Real: The Bankruptcy of a Romantic Realist," Bulletin of Ibaraki Christian Junior College, 21 (1981), 11-20.

493. Astro, Richard. "From the Tidepool to the Stars: S's Sense of Place," SQ, 10 (Winter 1977), 5-11; reprinted in JS: East and West (SMS, No. 8), T. Hayashi, et al., 1978. pp. 22-27.

494. _____. "Introduction" to S and the Sea, eds. R. Astro and Joel W. Hedgpeth, 1975. pp. 5-8.

495. _____. "Introduction" to S: The Man and His Work, eds. R. Astro and T. Hayashi, 1971. pp. 1-10.

496. _____. "JS and the Tragic Miracle of Consciousness," SJS, 1 (November 1975), 61-72.

497. _____. "Joseph Fontenrose: A Message," SQ, 6 (Spring 1973), 40-42.

498. _____. "Phlebas Sails the Caribbean: S, Hemingway, and the American Waste Land," The Twenties: Fiction, Poetry, Drama, ed. Warren French, 1976. pp. 215-33.

499. _____. "Something That Happened: A Non-Teleological Approach to 'The Leader of the People,'" SQ, 6

(Winter 1973), 19-23; reprinted in A Study Guide to S's "The Long Valley," ed. T. Hayashi, 1976. pp. 105-11.

500. _____. "S and Mainwaring: Two Californians for the Earth," S's Literary Dimension: A Guide to Comparative Studies, ed. T. Hayashi, 1973. pp. 83-93.

501. _____. "S and Ricketts: Escape or Commitment in the Sea of Cortez?" WAL, 6 (Summer 1971), 109-22.

502. _____. "S and Ricketts: The Morphology of a Metaphysic," University of Windsor R, 8 (Spring 1973), 24-33.

503. _____. "S Country (Editorial Preface)," SQ, 4 (Summer 1971), 67.

504. "No entry."

505. Astro, Richard. "S's Sea of Cortez (1941)," A Study Guide to S: A Handbook to His Major Works, ed. T. Hayashi, 1974. pp. 168-86.

506. _____. "Travels with S: The Laws of Thought and the Laws of Things," SQ, 8 (Spring 1975), 35-44; reprinted in S's Travel Literature (SMS, No. 10), ed. T. Hayashi, 1980. pp. 1-11.

507. Autrey, Max L. "Men, Mice, and Moths: Gradation in S's 'The Leader of the People,'" WAL, 10 (November 1975), 195-204.

508. Barbour, Brian M. "S as a Short Story Writer," A Study Guide to S's "The Long Valley," ed. T. Hayashi, 1976. pp. 113-28.

509. Beatty, Sandra. "S's Play-Women: A Study of the Female Presence in Of Mice and Men, Burning Bright, The Moon Is Down, and Viva Zapata!," S's Women (SMS, No. 9), ed. T. Hayashi, 1979. pp. 7-16.

510. _____. "A Study of Female Characterization in S's Fiction," S's Women (SMS, No. 9), ed. T. Hayashi, 1979. pp. 1-6.

511. Bedford, Richard C. "The Genesis and Consolation of Our Discontent," Criticism, 14 (Summer 1972), 277-94.

512. _____. "S's Bank Robbery Motif," Asphodel (Doshisha Women's College, Japan), 5 (July 1972), [n. p.].

513. _____. "S's Uses of the Oriental," Asphodel, 11 (1978), 48-75; also in SQ, 13 (Winter-Spring 1980), 5-19.

514. Bellman, Samuel I. "Control and Freedom in S's Of Mice and Men," CEA Critic, 38 (November 1975), 25-27.

515. Benardete, Jane. "S," American Realism: A Shape for Fiction. New York: Putnam, 1972. pp. 384-414.

516. Benson, Jackson J. "An Afterword and an Introduction," JML, 5 (April 1976), 194-216 [See also 336].

517. _____. "Environment as Meaning: JS and the Great Central Valley," SQ, 10 (Winter 1977), 12-20.

518. _____. "JS: Novelist as Scientist," S and the Sea, eds. R. Astro and J. W. Hedgpeth, 1975. pp. 15-28; reprinted in Novel, 10 (Spring 1977), 248-64.

519. _____. "JS's Cannery Row: A Reconsideration," WAL, 12 (May 1977), 11-40.

520. Benson, Jackson J., and Anne Loftis. "JS and Farm Labor Unionization: The Backgrounds of In Dubious Battle," AL, 52 (May 1980), 194-223.

521. Benton, Robert M. " 'Breakfast' I and II," A Study Guide to S's "The Long Valley," ed. T. Hayashi, 1976. pp. 33-39.

522. _____. "The Ecological Nature of Cannery Row," S: The Man and His Work, eds. R. Astro and T. Hayashi, 1971. pp. 131-39.

523. _____. "Realism, Growth, and Contrast in 'The Gift,'" SQ, 6 (Winter 1973), 3-9; reprinted in A Study Guide to S's "The Long Valley," ed. T. Hayashi, 1976. pp. 81-88.

524. _____. "A Scientific Point of View in S's Fiction,"
SQ, 7 (Summer-Fall 1974), 67-73.

525. _____. "S's The Long Valley (1938), A Study Guide
to S: A Handbook to His Major Works, ed. T. Hayashi, 1974. pp. 69-86.

526. Berry, J. Wilkes. "Enduring Life in The Grapes of
Wrath," CEA Critic 33 (1971), 18-19.

527. Beston, John B. "The Influence of JS's The Pastures
of Heaven on Patric White," Australian Literary
Studies (University of Tasmania), 6 (1974), 317-19.

528. Beyer, Preston. "JS: Selected Episodes," SQ, 12
(Summer-Fall 1979), 78-86.

529. _____. "S's Vanderbilt Clinic," SQ, 14 (Summer-
Fall 1981), 70-71.

530. _____. "A Tribute: Four Years of Success [Special
Message]," SQ, 5 (Winter 1972), 3-4.

531. Bluestone, George. "The Grapes of Wrath," in his
Novels into Films (Baltimore: Johns Hopkins University Press, 1957), pp. 147-69; reprinted in S:
A Collection of Critical Essays, ed. R. M. Davis,
1972. pp. 102-23; 20th Century Interpretations of
"The Grapes of Wrath," ed. R. C. Davis, 1982.
pp. 79-99.

532. Bode, Elroy. "S" in Home and Other Moments. El
Paso: Texas Western Press, 1975. pp. 132-44.

533. "No entry."

534. Bowden, Edwin T. "The Commonplace and the Grotesque," in his The Dungeon of the Heart. New York:
Macmillan, 1961, pp. 138-49; reprinted in excerpt
form in 20th Century Interpretations of "The Grapes
of Wrath," ed. R. C. Davis, 1982. pp. 15-23.

535. Brasch, James D. "The Grapes of Wrath and Old
Testament Skepticism," SJS, 3 (May 1977), 16-27.

536. Bredahl, A. Carl, Jr. "The Drinking Metaphor in The
Grapes of Wrath," SQ, 6 (Fall 1973), 95-98.

537. Brown, Joyce C. "S's East of Eden." Explicator, 38 (Fall 1979), 11-12.

538. Bunzel, John H. "Welcoming Address [at the S Conference and Film Festival]," SQ, 4 (Summer 1971), 69-73.

539. Burns, Stuart L. "The Turtle or the Gopher: Another Look at the Ending of The Grapes of Wrath," WAL, 9 (May 1974), 53-57; reprinted in 20th Century Interpretations of "The Grapes of Wrath," ed. R. C. Davis, 1982. pp. 100-04.

540. Caldwell, Mary Ellen. "A New Consideration of the Intercalary Chapters in The G of W," Markham R, 3 (May 1973), 115-19; reprinted in 20th Century Interpretations of "The Grapes of Wrath," ed. R. C. Davis, 1982. pp. 105-14.

541. Callow, James T., and Robert J. Reilly. "JS," Guide to American Literature from Emily Dickinson to the Present. New York: Barnes and Noble, 1977. pp. 138-41.

542. Campbell, A. M. "Reports from Weedpatch, California; the Records of the Farm Security Administration," Agricultural History, 48 (July 1974), 402-04.

543. Campbell, Russell. "Tramping Out the Vintage: Sour Grapes," in The Modern American Novel and the Movies, eds. Gerald Peary and Roger Shotzkin. New York: Ungar, 1978. pp. 107-18 [The Grapes of Wrath].

544. Carlson, Eric W. "Symbolism in The Grapes of Wrath," College English, 19 (January 1958), 172-75; reprinted in JS: "The Grapes of Wrath": Text and Criticism, ed. P. Lisca, 1972. pp. 748-56.

545. Carpenter, Frederic I. "The Philosophical Joads," College English, 2 (January 1941), 315-25; reprinted in JS: "The Grapes of Wrath": Text and Criticism, ed. P. Lisca, 1972. pp. 708-19.

546. Carr, Duane R. "S's Blakean Vision in The Grapes of Wrath," SQ, 8 (Summer-Fall 1975), 67-73.

547. Carter, Tom. "S Country, " Ford Times, 68 (March 1975), 3-7.

548. Caselli, Jaclyn. "JS and the American Patchwork Quilt, " SJS 1 (November 1975), 83-87.

549. Champney, Freeman. "JS, Californian, " Antioch R, 7 (September 1947), 345-62; reprinted in S: A Collection of Critical Essays, ed. R. M. Davis, 1972. pp. 18-35.

550. Chandra, Naresh. "JS's The Winter of Our Discontent: Continuity of a Theme, " Indiana Journal of English Studies, 3 (1973) [n. p.].

551. Chen, Ching-Chi. "A Plot Analysis of The Grapes of Wrath, " Kaohsiung Teachers College Journal (Taiwan), 5 (January 1977), 63-126.

552. Clancy, Charles J. "Light in The Winter of Our Discontent, " SQ, 9 (Summer-Fall 1976), 91-101.

553. _____. "S's The Moon Is Down (1942), " A Study Guide to S (Part II), ed. T. Hayashi, 1979. pp. 100-21.

554. _____. "S's A Russian Journal (1948), " A Study Guide to S. (Part II), ed. T. Hayashi, 1979. pp. 122-38; S's Travel Literature (SMS, No. 10), ed. T. Hayashi, 1980. pp. 38-46.

555. Cobbs, Lewis E. "Maupassant's 'Idylle': A Source for S's The Grapes of Wrath, " Notes on Modern American Literature, 3 (1978), Item 1.

556. Cole, Gloria. "S and Hemingway: The Women Behind Them, " Fairpress (Westport, Conn.), November 3, 1976. 9B, 12B.

557. Collins, Thomas A. "From Bringing in the Sheaves, by 'Windsor Drake' with a Foreword by JS, " JML, 5 (April 1976), 211-32.

558. Cook, Bruce. "Monterey Is Still S Country, " National Observer. July 13, 1974. p. 20.

559. Cook, Sylvia. "S, the People, and the Party, " SQ, 15 (Winter-Spring 1982), 11-23 [The Grapes of Wrath].

560. _____. "S's Retreat into Artfulness," From Tobacco
Road to Route 66: The Southern Poor White in Fic-
tion. Chapel Hill: University of North Carolina
Press, 1976. pp. 153-83.

561. Copek, Peter. "JS and Feeling in Fiction," S and the
Sea, eds. R. Astro and J. W. Hedgpeth, 1975. pp.
45-57.

562. _____. "S's 'Naturalism'?," SQ, 9 (Winter 1976),
9-12.

563. Court, Franklin E. "S's Of Mice and Men (Play)
(1937)," A Study Guide to S: A Handbook to His
Major Works, ed. T. Hayashi, 1974. pp. 155-67.

564. _____. "A Vigilante's Fantasy," SQ, 5 (Summer-
Fall 1972), 98-101; reprinted in A Study Guide to
S's "The Long Valley," ed. T. Hayashi, 1976. pp.
53-56.

565. Covoci, Pascal, Jr. "Introduction" to The Portable
S, ed. P. Covoci, Jr. New York: Viking Press,
1971. pp. xi-xxix.

566. _____. "S's Quest for Magnanimity," SQ, 10 (Summer-Fall 1977), 79-89.

567. _____. "Work and the Timeliness of The Grapes of
Wrath," JS: "The Grapes of Wrath": Text and
Criticism, ed. P. Lisca, 1972. pp. 814-24.

568. Cowley, Malcolm. "What Books Survive from the
1930s?" Journal of American Studies, 7 (December
1973), 3.

569. Cox, Martha Heasley. "The Conclusion of The Grapes
of Wrath: S's Conception and Execution," SJS, 1
(November 1975), 73-81.

570. _____. "Environment as Meaning in JS's Work,"
SQ, 10 (Winter 1977), 4-5.

571. _____. "Fact into Fiction in The Grapes of Wrath:
The Weedpatch and Arvin Camps," JS: East and
West (SMS, No. 8), ed. T. Hayashi, et al., 1978.
pp. 12-21.

572. _____. "In Search of JS: His People and His Land,"
SJS, 1 (November 1975), 73-81.

573. _____. "The JS Society Meeting at the 1975 MLA
Convention," SQ, 10 (Winter 1977), 4.

574. _____. "Remembering JS," SJS, 1 (November 1975),
73-81.

575. _____. "S Country: A Conference and Film Festival," SQ, 4 (Summer 1971), 68.

576. _____. "S's Burning Bright (1950)," A Study Guide
to S (Part II), ed. T. Hayashi, 1979. pp. 46-62.

577. _____. "S's Cup of Gold (1929)," A Study Guide to
S (Part II), ed. T. Hayashi, 1979. pp. 19-45.

578. _____. "S's The Pearl (1947)," A Study Guide to S:
A Handbook to His Major Works, ed. T. Hayashi,
1974. pp. 107-28.

579. _____. "A Time to Remember," SQ, 10 (Spring
1977), 48-49 [First International S. Congress, 1976].

580. Davac, Lee. "Lennie as Christian in Of Mice and
Men," Southwestern American Literature, 4 (1974)
87-91.

581. Davis, Robert Con. "Introduction" to Twentieth Cen-
tury Interpretations of "The Grapes of Wrath," ed.
R. C. Davis. Englewood Cliffs, N. J.: Prentice-
Hall, 1982. pp. 1-11.

582. Davis, Robert Murray. "Introduction" to S: A Collection of Critical Essays, ed. R. M. Davis, 1972.
pp. 1-17.

583. _____. "S's "The Murder,'" Studies in Short Fiction,
14 (Winter 1977), 63-68.

584. Degan, James P. "In Definite Battle: S and California's Land Monopolists," S: The Man and His Work,
ed. R. Astro and T. Hayashi, 1971. pp. 65-74.

585. DeMott, Robert. "Cathy Ames and Lady Godiva: A
Contribution to East of Eden's Background," SQ, 14
(Summer-Fall 1981), 72-83.

585a. _____. " 'Calling All Books': S's Reading and East of Eden, " SQ, 14 (Winter-Spring 1981), 40-51.

586. _____. " 'A Great Black Book': East of Eden and Gunn's New Family Physician, " American Studies, 22 (Fall 1981), 41-57.

587. _____. "The Interior Distances of JS, " SQ, 12 (Summer-Fall 1979), 86-99.

588. _____. "The JS Society Meeting at the 1976 MLA Convention, " SQ, 10 (Summer-Fall 1977), 68.

589. _____. "S and the Creative Process: First Manifesto to End the Bringdown Against Sweet Thursday, " S: The Man and His Work, ed. R. Astro and T. Hayashi, 1971. pp. 157-78.

590. _____. "S's To a God Unknown (1933), " A Study Guide to His Major Works, ed. T. Hayashi, 1974. pp. 187-213.

591. _____. "Toward a Redefinition of To a God Unknown, " University of Windsor R, 8 (Spring 1973), 34-53.

592. Ditsky, John. "Between Acrobats and Seals: S in the U. S. S. R. , " SQ, 15 (Winter-Spring 1982), 23-29 [S's A Russian Journal, 1949, and Arthur Miller and Inge Morath's In Russia, 1969].

593. _____. "A Call for Critics, " SQ, 9 (Summer-Fall 1976), 84-85.

594. _____. " 'Directionality': The Compass in the Heart, " in The Westering Experience in American Literature, eds. M. Lewis and L. L. Lee, 1977. pp. 215-20.

595. _____. "The 'East' in East of Eden, " JS: East and West (SMS, No. 8), eds. T. Hayashi, et al. , 1978. pp. 61-70.

596. _____. "The Ending of The Grapes of Wrath, " Agora (State University of N. Y. at Potsdam), 2 (Fall 1973), 41-50.

597. _____. "Faulkner and S: Men and the Land," S's Literary Dimension: A Guide to Comparative Studies, ed. T. Hayashi, 1973. pp. 28-45.

598. _____. "Faulkner Land and S. Country," S: The Man and His Work, eds. R. Astro and T. Hayashi, 1971. pp. 11-23.

599. _____. "The Grapes of Wrath: A Reconsideration," Southern Humanities R, 13 (Summer 1979), 215-20.

600. _____. "JS, 1902-1968 [Introduction to Special S Issue]," University of Windsor R, 8 (Spring 1973), 5.

601. _____. "Music from a Dark Cave: Organic Form in S's Fiction," Journal of Narrative Technique, 1 (1970), 59-67.

602. _____. "The 1978 MLA S Society Meeting Papers: An Introduction," SQ, 12 (Summer-Fall 1979), 77-78.

603. _____. "Outside of Paradise: Men and the Land in His East of Eden," Essays on "East of Eden" (SMS, No. 7), 1977. pp. 15-40.

604. _____. "Ritual Murder in S's Dramas," SQ, 11 (Summer-Fall 1978), 72-76.

605. _____. "S's Bombs Away: The Group-man in the Wild Blue Yonder," SQ, 12 (Winter-Spring 1979), 5-14.

606. _____. "S's Burning Bright: Homage to Astarte," SQ, 7 (Summer-Fall 1974), 79-84.

607. _____. "S's 'Flight': The Ambiguity of Manhood," SQ, 5 (Summer-Fall 1972), 80-85; reprinted in A Study Guide to S's "The Long Valley," ed. T. Hayashi, 1976. pp. 17-23.

608. _____. "S's Travels with Charley: The Quest That Failed," SQ, 8 (Spring 1975), 45-50; reprinted in S's Travel Literature (SMS, No. 10), ed. T. Hayashi, 1980. pp. 56-61.

609. _____. "Teaching the Ungreat: A Year of S,"
English R, 22 (1972), 41-50.

610. _____. "Towards A Narrational Self," Essays on
"East of Eden" (SMS, No. 7), 1977. pp. 1-14.

611. _____. "The Wayward Bus: Love and Time in
America," SJS, 1 (November 1975), 89-101; re-
printed in S's Travel Literature (SMS, No. 10), ed.
T. Hayashi, 1980. pp. 61-75.

612. _____. "The Winter of Our Discontent: S's Testament on Naturalism," Research Studies, 44 (March
1976), 42-51.

613. _____. "With S in Japan," SQ, 10 (Spring 1977),
50-52.

614. _____. "Words and Deeds in Viva Zapata!," Dalhousie R, 56 (1976), 125-31.

615. Donald, Miles. "The Traditional Novel," The American Novel in the Twentieth Century. New York:
Barnes and Noble, 1978. pp. 59-72 [The Grapes
of Wrath].

616. Downs, Robert B. "Okies and Arkies," in his Famous
American Books. New York: McGraw-Hill, 1971.
pp. 311-19.

617. Dunbar, Maurice. "Burning Bright by JS," SQ, 13
(Winter-Spring 1980), 44-45.

618. _____. "Collecting S," SQ, 12 (Winter-Spring 1979),
42-48; reprinted in A Handbook for S Collectors,
Librarians, and Scholars (SMS, No. 11), ed. T.
Hayashi, 1981. pp. 19-23.

619. _____. "JS" in his Books and Collectors. Los
Altos, Cal.: Book Nest, 1980. Passim.

620. _____. "JS in his Fundamentals of Book Collecting.
Los Altos, Cal.: Hermes, 1976. pp. 23-24.

621. Eddy, Darlene. "To Go A-Buccaneering and Take a
Spanish Town: Some Seventeenth-Century Aspects
of Cup of Gold," SQ, 8 (Winter 1975), 3-12; re-

printed as "Some 17th-Century Aspects of Cup of Gold," S's Travel Literature (SMS, No. 10), ed. T. Hayashi, 1980. pp. 27-38.

622. Eisinger, Chester E. "Jeffersonian Agrarianism in The Grapes of Wrath," University of Kansas City R, 14 (Winter 1947), 149-54; reprinted in JS: "The Grapes of Wrath": Text and Criticism, ed. P. Lisca, 1972. pp. 720-28.

623. Ek, Grete. " 'A Speaking Picture' in JS's The Grapes of Wrath," American Studies in Scandinavia, 10 (1978), 111-15.

624. Elliot, Kathleen Farr. "S's 'IITYWYBAD,' " SQ, 6 (Spring 1973), 53-54 [The Grapes of Wrath].

625. Everson, William K. "S," Archetype West: The Pacific Coast as a Literary Region. Berkeley, Cal.: Oyez, 1976. pp. 83-99.

626. _____. "Thoughts on a Great Adaptation," in The Modern American Novels and the Movies, eds. Gerald Peary and Roger Shotzkin. New York: Ungar, 1978. pp. 63-69 [Of Mice and Men].

627. Falkenberg, Sandra. "A Study of Female Characterization in S's Fiction," SQ, 8 (Spring 1975), 50-56.

628. "February Is S Month in S Country," Sunset, 162 (February 1979), 44-45.

629. Federle, Steven J. "Lifeboat as Allegory: S and the Demon of War," SQ, 12 (Winter-Spring 1979), 14-20.

630. Fitzpatrick, Joe. "My Bag," Monterey Peninsula Herald, July 31, 1971. p. 10.

631. Fontenrose, Joseph. "The Grapes of Wrath," in JS: An Introduction and Interpretation by Joseph Fontenrose. New York: Holt, Rinehart and Winston, 1963, pp. 67-83; reprinted in JS: "The Grapes of Wrath": Text and Criticism, ed. P. Lisca, 1972. pp. 784-800.

632. _____. " 'The Harness'," SQ, 5 (Summer-Fall 1972),

94-98; reprinted in A Study Guide to S's "The Long Valley", ed. T. Hayashi, 1976. pp. 47-52.

633. _____. "Introduction" to S and the Arthurian Theme (SMS, No. 5), ed. T. Hayashi, 1975. pp. 1-3.

634. _____. "Sea of Cortez, " in his JS: An Introduction and Interpretation. New York: Holt, Rinehart and Winston, 1963, pp. 84-97; reprinted in S: A Collection of Critical Essays, ed. R. M. Davis, 1972. pp. 122-34.

635. Fossey, W. Richard. "The End of the Western Dream: The Grapes of Wrath and Oklahoma, " Cimarron R (Oklahoma State University), 22 (1973), 25-34.

636. French, Warren. "After The Grapes of Wrath, " SQ, 8 (Summer-Fall 1975), 73-78.

637. _____. "The 'California Quality' of S's Best Fiction, " SJS, 1 (November 1975), 9-19.

638. _____. "End of a Dream, " JS. New York: Twayne, 1961, pp. 72-79; reprinted in S: A Collection of Critical Essays, ed. R. M. Davis, 1972. pp. 63-69.

639. _____. "Foreword: The Artist as Magician, " A Study Guide to S: A Handbook to His Major Works, ed. T. Hayashi, 1974. pp. xiii-xvi.

640. _____. "From Naturalism to the Drama of Consciousness: The Education of the Heart in The Grapes of Wrath, " JS. Boston: Twayne, 1975, pp. 92-102; reprinted in 20th Century Interpretations of "The Grapes of Wrath, " ed. R. C. Davis, 1982. pp. 24-35.

641. _____. "Homage to Joseph Fontenrose, " SQ, 6 (Spring 1973), 38-40.

642. _____. "In Memoriam: Lawrence William Jones, " SQ, 4 (Spring 1971), 35.

643. _____. "Introduction, " SQ, 9 (Winter 1976), 8-9 [Naturalism].

644. _____. "Introduction" to JS: East and West (SMS, No. 8), eds. T. Hayashi, et al., 1978. pp. ix-xii.

645. _____. "Introduction" to S and Hemingway: Dissertation Abstracts and Research Opportunities, ed. T. Hayashi, 1980. pp. xi-xiv.

646. _____. "JS," The Politics of Twentieth-Century Novelists, ed. George Andrew Panichas. New York: Hawthorn Books, 1971. pp. 296-306.

647. _____. "JS and Modernism: A Speculation on His Contribution to the Development of the 20th Century American Sensibility," S's Prophetic Vision of America, eds. T. Hayashi and K. D. Swan, 1976. pp. 35-55.

648. _____. "JS: A Usable Concept of Naturalism," American Literary Naturalism: A Reassessment, eds. Yoshinobu Hakutani and Lewis Fried. Heidelberg, Germany: Carl Winter, 1975. pp. 122-35.

649. _____. "The JS Society Meeting at the 1974 MLA Convention," SQ, 9 (Winter 1976), 8.

650. _____. "JS," Twentieth-Century American Literature. New York: St. Martin's, 1980. pp. 556-60.

651. "No entry."

652. French, Warren. " 'Johnny Bear'--S's 'Yellow Peril' Story," SQ, 5 (Summer-Fall 1972), 101-07; reprinted in A Study Guide to S's "The Long Valley," ed. T. Hayashi, 1976. pp. 57-64.

653. _____. "Marston LaFrance, 1927-1975," SQ, 9 (Winter 1976), 4-6.

654. "No entry."

655. French, Warren. "The Moon Is Down: JS's 'Times'," SQ, 11 (Summer-Fall 1978), 77-87.

656. _____. "Political Context of the JS Stamp," SQ, 12 (Summer-Fall 1979), 69-74.

657. _____. "Presidential Message," SQ, 5 (Winter 1972), 6-7.

658. _____. "Presidential Message: S and Modernism,"
SQ, 9 (Summer-Fall 1976), 69-71.

659. _____. "President's Special Message," SQ, 11
(Summer-Fall 1978), 69-72.

660. _____. "Presidential Message," SQ, 12 (Summer-
Fall 1979), 69-74.

661. _____. See his annual reviews of S publications in
American Literary Scholarship/An Annual. Durham,
N. C.: Duke University Press, 1971-73 [See also
O'Connor, Margaret (1974-77) and Salzman, Jack
(1978-)].

662. _____. "JS," Dictionary of Literary Biography. IX,
247-71.

663. _____. "S and Salinger: Messiah-Moulders for a
Sick Society," S's Literary Dimension: A Guide to
Comparative Studies, ed. T. Hayashi, 1973. pp.
105-15.

664. _____. "S's The Grapes of Wrath (1939)," A Study
Guide to S: A Handbook to His Major Works, ed.
T. Hayashi, 1974. pp. 29-46.

665. _____. "S's Use of Malory," S and the Arthurian
Theme (SMS, No. 5), ed. T. Hayashi, 1975. pp.
4-11.

666. Garcia, Reloy. "Introduction" to A Study Guide to S
(Part II), ed. T. Hayashi, 1979. pp. 4-5.

667. _____. "Introduction" to A Study Guide to S's "The
Long Valley", ed. T. Hayashi, 1976. pp. xii-xiv.

668. _____. "JS's Bicentennial America," SQ, 9 (Summer-
Fall 1976), 86-88.

669. _____. "The Rocky Road to Eldorado: The Journey
Motif in JS's The Grapes of Wrath," SQ 14 (Summer-
Fall 1981), 83-93.

670. _____. "S's 'The Snake': An Explication," SQ, 5
(Summer-Fall 1972), 85-90; reprinted in A Study
Guide to S's "The Long Valley," ed. T. Hayashi,
1976. pp. 25-31.

671. _____. "S's The Winter of Our Discontent (1961),"
     A Study Guide to S: A Handbook to His Major
     Works, ed. T. Hayashi, 1974. pp. 244-57.

672. Gide, André. "In Dubious Battle," Journal of André
     Gide, IV, 1939-49, tr. Justin M. O'Brien. New
     York: Knopf, 1951, p. 48; reprinted in S: A Col-
     lection of Critical Essays, ed. R. M. Davis, 1972.
     pp. 47-48.

673. Gladstein, Mimi Reisel. "Female Characters in S:
     Minor Characters of Major Importance?" S's Wom-
     en (SMS, No. 9), ed. T. Hayashi, 1979. pp. 17-
     26.

674. _____. "Ma Joad and Pilar: Significantly Similar,"
     SQ, 14 (Summer-Fall 1981), 93-104.

675. _____. "S's Juana: A Woman of Worth," SQ, 9
     (Winter 1976), 20-24; reprinted in S's Women (SMS,
     No. 9), ed. T. Hayashi, 1979. pp. 49-52.

676. Goldhurst, William. "Of Mice and Men: JS's Parable
     of the Curse of Cain," WAL, 6 (Summer 1971), 123-
     36.

677. Goldsmith, Arnold L. "Thematic Rhythm in The Red
     Pony," College English, 26 (February 1965), 391-94;
     reprinted in S: A Collection of Critical Essays, ed.
     R. M. Davis, 1972. pp. 70-74.

677a. Govoni, Mark W. " 'Symbols for the Wordlessness':
     The Original Manuscript of East of Eden," SQ, 14
     (Winter-Spring 1981), 14-23.

678. Gray, James. "JS," Seven Novelists in the American
     Naturalist Tradition, ed. Charles Child Walcutt.
     Minneapolis: University of Minneapolis Press, 1974.
     pp. 205-44.

679. Gribben, John. "S's East of Eden and Milton's Para-
     dise Lost: A Discussion of Timshel," SQ, 5 (Spring
     1972), 35-43; reprinted in S's Literary Dimension:
     A Guide to Comparative Studies, ed. T. Hayashi,
     1973. pp. 94-104.

680. Griffin, Robert J., and William A. Freedman. "Ma-

chines and Animals: Pervasive Motifs in The Grapes of Wrath," Journal of English and Germanic Philosophy, 62 (April 1963), 569-80; reprinted in JS: "The Grapes of Wrath: Text and Criticism, ed. P. Lisca, 1972. pp. 769-83; 20th Century Interpretations of "The Grapes of Wrath," ed. R. C. Davis, 1982. pp. 115-27.

681. Groene, Horst. "Agrarianism and Technology in S's The G of W," Southern R, 9 (1976), 27-32; reprinted in 20th Century Interpretations of "The G of W," ed. R. C. Davis, 1982. pp. 128-33.

682. _____. "The Themes of Manliness and Human Dignity in S's Story, 'Flight,' " Die Neueren Sprachen, 72 (1973), 278-84.

683. Guerin, Wilfred, et al. "The Snake," Instructor's Manual to Accompany "Mandala" Literature for Critical Analysis." New York: Harper & Row, 1970. pp. 75-77.

683a. Gunn, Drewey Wayne. "The End of an Era," American and British Writers in Mexico, 1956-1973. Austin: University of Texas Press, 1974. pp. 197-204.

684. Gurko, Leo. "Of Mice and Men: S as Manichean," University of Windsor R, 8 (Spring 1973), 11-23.

685. Hamaguchi, Osamu. "Idiot Lennie in Of Mice and Men," Chu-Shikoku Studies in American Literature, 11 (January 1975) [n. p.].

686. _____. "Theme and Technique of Of Mice and Men," Phoenix (Japan), 14 (February 1978), 171-84.

687. Hamby, James A. "S's Biblical Vision: 'Breakfast' and the Nobel Acceptance Speech," Western R, 10 (Spring 1973), 57-59.

688. _____. "S's The Pearl: Tradition and Innovation," Western R, 7 (Winter 1970), 65-66.

689. Hargrave, John. "S and Summer Time Ends," SQ, 6 (Summer 1973), 67-73.

690. "No entry."

691. Hayashi, Tetsumaro. "A Chronology of the JS Society of America: The First Ten Years (1966-1975)," SQ, 9 (Summer-Fall 1976), 72-83.

692. _____. "Elizabeth R. Otis as I Remember Her," SQ 15 (Winter-Spring 1982), 6-8.

693. _____. "In Memory of Marston LaFrance," SQ, 9 (Winter 1976), 4.

694. _____. "Introduction" [to Articles Devoted to S's Short Stories in The Long Valley], SQ, 5 (Summer-Fall 1972), 67-68.

695. _____. "Joseph Fontenrose: Biography and Bibliography," SQ, 6 (Spring 1973), 35-36.

696. _____. "The Pearl as the Novel of Disengagement," 7 (Summer-Fall 1974), 84-88.

697. _____. "Scholars and Collectors: How a S Scholar Views S Collectors," A Handbook for S Collectors, Librarians, and Scholars (SMS, No. 11), ed. T. Hayashi, 1981. pp. 6-7.

698. _____. "S's Prophetic Vision," S's Prophetic Vision of America, eds. T. Hayashi and K. D. Swan, 1976. pp. 10-11.

699. _____. "S's Reputation: What Values Does He Communicate to Us?" S's Prophetic Vision of America, eds. T. Hayashi and K. D. Swan, 1976. pp. 28-34.

700. _____. "S's Winter as Shakespearean Fiction," SQ, 12 (Summer-Fall 1979), 107-15.

701. _____. "S's Women in The Grapes of Wrath: A New Perspective," KAL, 18 (October 1977), 1-4.

702. _____. "The Theme of Revolution in Julius Caesar and Viva Zapata!," JS: East and West (SMS, No. 8), eds. T. Hayashi, et al., 1978. pp. 28-39.

703. _____. "A Tribute to Dr. Joseph Fontenrose," SQ, 6 (Spring 1973), 35.

704. _____. "Why Is S's Literature Widely Read? What

Is the Essence of His Literature?" <u>KAL</u>, 20 (September 1979), 42-44; reprinted in "Why Is S's Literature Widely Read?," <u>SQ</u>, 13 (Winter-Spring 1980), 20-23.

705. Hayman, Lee Richard. "Report from Salinas (I)," <u>SQ</u>, 3 (Spring 1970), 43-44; (II), <u>SQ</u>, 12 (Summer-Fall 1979), 74-76.

706. _____. "S's Birthday and Commemorative Stamp Celebration in Salinas, California," <u>SQ</u>, 12 (Summer-Fall 1979), 74-76.

707. Hedgpeth, Joel W. "Escape from Salinas," <u>S and the Sea</u>, eds. R. Astro and J. W. Hedgpeth, 1975. pp. 9-10.

708. _____. "Genesis of the <u>Sea of Cortez</u>," <u>SQ</u>, 6 (Summer 1973), 74-80.

709. _____. "Philosophy on Cannery Row," <u>S: The Man and His Work</u>, eds. R. Astro and T. Hayashi, 1971. pp. 89-129.

710. Hedrick, Joan. "Mother Earth and Earth Mother: The Recasting of Myth in S's <u>The G of W</u>," <u>20th Century Interpretations of "The Grapes of Wrath</u>," ed. R. C. Davis, 1982. pp. 134-43.

711. Hirose, Hidekazu. "Feelings as Always Were More Potent Than Thought--JS's Social Concern in the Thirties," <u>Chu-Shikoku Studies in American Literature</u> (Japan), 8 (1972), 53-62.

712. _____. "From Doc Burton to Jim Casy: S in the Latter Half of the 1930s," <u>JS: East and West</u> (SMS, No. 8), eds. T. Hayashi, et al., 1978. pp. 6-11.

713. Hodges, Laura F. "Arthur, Lancelot, and the Psychodrama of S," <u>SQ</u>, 13 (Summer-Fall 1980), 71-79.

714. _____. "The Personae of Acts: Symbolic Repetition and Variation," <u>SQ</u>, 12 (Winter-Spring 1979), 20-27.

715. Hopfe, Lewis Moore. "Genesis Imagery in S," <u>Cresset</u>, 39 (May 1976), 6-9.

716. Hopkins, Karen J. "S's East of Eden: A Defense,"
      Essays on California Writers (Itinerary 7), ed.
      Charles L. Crow. Bowling Green University Press,
      1978. pp. 63-78.

717. Hughes, Robert S., Jr. "S Stories at the Houghton
      Library: A Case for Authenticity of Four Unpub-
      lished Texts," Harvard Library Bulletin, 30 (Jan-
      uary 1982), 87-95 ["The Days of Long Marsh,"
      "East Third Street," "The Nail," and "The Nymph
      and Isobel" (See Lewis, Clifford L.)].

718. Hunter, J. Paul. "S's Wine of Affirmation in The
      Grapes of Wrath," Essays in Modern American
      Literature, eds. Richard E. Langford, et al. De-
      Land, Fla.: Stetson University Press, 1963; re-
      printed in JS: "The Grapes of Wrath": Text and
      Criticism, ed. P. Lisca, 1972. pp. 801-13; re-
      printed in 20th Century Interpretations of "The
      Grapes of Wrath," ed. R. C. Davis, 1982. pp.
      36-47.

719. Imanaga, Iwao. "A Short Survey of JS's Style," Nippon
      University Literature and Sciences Research Report,
      25 (February 1977), 189-208.

720. "Interview with JS," Paris R, 63 (Fall 1975), 180-94
      (anonymous).

721. Iseri, Ryujoh. "JS's Non-teleological Thinking," KAL,
      17 (September 1976), 77-82.

722. Izu, Taiwa. "S and The Winter of Our Discontent,"
      Journal of the Faculty of Liberal Arts (Yamaguchi
      University, Japan), 5 (November 1971) [n. p.].

723. Jain, Sunita. "The Concept of Man in the Novels of
      JS," Journal of School of Language, 3 (1975), 98-
      102.

724. Jay, Herman. "Hollywood and American Literature:
      The American Novel on the Screen," English Journal,
      66 (1975), 82-86 [East of Eden and The Grapes of
      Wrath].

725. Johnston, Kenneth G. "Teaching the Short Story: An
      Approach to S's 'Flight,' " Kansas English, 58 (1973),
      4-11.

726. Jones, Lawrence W. " 'A Little Play in Your Head': Parable Form in JS's Post-War Fiction, " Genre, 3 (1970), 55-63.

727. _____. "Poison in the Cream Puff: The Human Condition in Cannery Row, " SQ, 7 (Spring 1974), 35-40.

728. _____. "S and Zola: Theory and Practice of the Experimental Novel, " S's Literary Dimension: A Guide to Comparative Studies, ed. T. Hayashi, 1973. pp. 138-46.

729. _____. "Whole Life and the Holy Life: JS and the Riddle of Belief, " Religion in Life, 39 (Winter 1970), 559-66.

730. Kaida, Koichi. "The Get-One Constructions in JS's Works, " Research Report of Yatsushiro National College of Technology, 3 (1981) [n. p.].

730a. _____. "The Language Feature of Migrant Workers in and Around Oklahoma in the 1930s--Based on The Grapes of Wrath, " KAL, 7 (September 1976), 83-84.

731. Kallapur, S. T. "The Grapes of Wrath: A Reapprais-al, " Indian Studies in American Literature. New York: Macmillan, 1974 [n. p.].

732. "No entry. "

733. _____. "JS and Oriental Thought, " The Images of India in Western Creative Writing, eds. M. K. Naik, et al. Dharmani: Karnatak University, 1971 [n. p.].

734. Kanfer, Stefan. "Brute Strength: Of Mice and Men by JS, " Time, 104 (December 30, 1974), 53.

735. Karinthy, Ferenc. "S and Zelk, " New Hungarian Quar-terly, 67 (1977), 103-07.

736. Kasahara, Masao. "On JS's Ubiquitous Use of Apt Alliterations in his America and Americans, " Kago-shima Studies in English Language and Literature, 2 (1971), [n. p.].

737. Kauffmann, Stanley. "Of Mice and Men," Persons of the Drama. New York: Harper & Row, 1976. pp. 156-59.

738. Kinney, Arthur F. "The Arthurian Cycle in Tortilla Flat," MFS, 11 (Spring 1965), 11-20; reprinted in S: A Collection of Critical Essays, ed. R. M. Davis, 1972. pp. 36-46.

739. _____. "Tortilla Flat Re-Visited," S and the Arthurian Theme (SMS, No. 5), ed. T. Hayashi, 1975. pp. 12-24.

740. Kline, Herbert. "On JS," SQ, 4 (Summer 1971), 80-88.

741. Knickerbocker, Brad. "S: Native Son Loses Prodigal-Son Image," Christian Science Monitor (Midwestern ed.), February 27, 1978. pp. 1, 30.

742. Kraft, Stephanie. No Castles on Main Street: American Authors and Their Homes. Chicago: Rand McNally, 1979. "S," pp. 85-93.

743. Krause, Sydney J. "The Pearl and 'Hadleyburg': From Desire to Renunciation," SQ, 7 (Winter 1974), 3-18.

744. _____. "S and Mark Twain," SQ, 6 (Fall 1973), 104-11.

745. Labric, Rodrique E. "American Naturalism: An Appraisal," Markham R, 2 (February 1971), 88-90.

746. LeMaster, J. R. "Mythological Constructs in S's To a God Unknown," Forum (Houston), 9 (Summer 1971), 8-11.

747. Levant, Howard. "JS's The Red Pony: A Study in Narrative Technique," Journal of Narrative Technique, 1 (1971), 77-85.

748. _____. "Tortilla Flat: The Shape of JS's Career," PMLA, 85 (October 1970), 1087-95.

749. _____. "The Unity of In Dubious Battle: Violence and Dehumanization," MFS, 11 (Spring 1965), 21-33; reprinted in S: A Collection of Critical Essays, ed. R. M. Davis, 1972. pp. 49-62.

750. Levathes, Kiki. "The JS Letters: 'Unconscious Autobiography'," New York Daily News. July 28, 1974
[n. p.].

751. Lewis, Clifford L. "Critical Perspectives on JS's Fiction," American Examiner, 6 (Fall-Winter 1978-
1979), 69-86.

752. _____. "Four Dubious S Stories," SQ, 5 (Winter
1972), 17-19 ["The Days of Long Marsh," "East
Third Street," "The Nail," and "The Nymph and
Isobel"]. See Hughes, Robert S., Jr.

753. _____. "The Grapes of Wrath: The Psychological
Transition from Clan to Community," American
Examiner, 6 (Fall-Winter 1978-1979), 40-68.

754. _____. "Jungian Psychology and the Artistic Design
of JS," SQ, 10 (Summer-Fall 1977), 89-97.

755. Lewis, R. W. B. "JS: The Fitful Daemon," The
Young Rebel in American Literature, ed. Carl Bode.
London: Heinemann, 1959, 121-41; reprinted in S:
A Collection of Critical Essays, ed. R. M. Davis,
1972. pp. 163-75.

756. _____. "The Picaresque Saint," Picaresque Saint.
New York: Lippincott, 1958, pp. 181-86; reprinted in
20th Century Interpretations of "The Grapes of
Wrath," ed. R. C. Davis, 1982. pp. 144-49.

757. _____. "Still Burning Bright," SR, 59 (October 18,
1975), 11-12.

758. Lieber, Todd M. "Talismanic Patterns in the Novels
of JS," AL, 44 (May 1972), 262-75.

759. Lisca, Peter. "Cannery Row and the Tao Teh Ching,"
SJS, 1 (November 1975), 21-27.

760. _____. "A Class at Berkeley," SQ, 6 (Spring 1973),
36-38 [Joseph Fontenrose].

761. _____. "Cup of Gold and To a God Unknown: Two
Early Works of JS," Kwartalinik Neofilolgiczny, 12
(February 1975), 174-83.

762. _____. "The Dynamics of Community in The Grapes of Wrath," in From Irving to S: Studies of American Literature in Honor of Harry R. Warfel, eds. Motley Deakin and P. Lisca. Gainesville: University of Florida Press, 1972. pp. 129-40.

763. _____. "Escape and Commitment: Two Poles of the S Hero," S: The Man and His Work, eds. R. Astro and T. Hayashi, 1971. pp. 75-88.

764. _____. "The Grapes of Wrath," in his The Wide World of JS. New Brunswick, N. J.: Rutgers University Press, 1958. pp. 144-77; reprinted in S: A Collection of Critical Essays, ed. R. M. Davis, 1972. pp. 75-101.

765. _____. "The Grapes of Wrath: An Achievement of Genius," in his JS: Nature and Myth. New York: Crowell, 1978. pp. 78-119; reprinted in 20th Century Interpretations of "The Grapes of Wrath," ed. R. C. Davis, 1982. pp. 48-62.

766. _____. "The Grapes of Wrath as Fiction," PMLA, 72 (March 1957), 296-309; reprinted in JS: "The Grapes of Wrath": Text and Criticism, ed. P. Lisca, 1972. pp. 729-47.

767. _____. "'The Raid' and In Dubious Battle," SQ, 5 (Summer-Fall 1972), 90-94; reprinted in A Study Guide to S's "The Long Valley," ed. T. Hayashi, 1976. pp. 41-45.

768. _____. "S and Hemingway: Suggestions for a Comparative Study," SQ, 2 (Spring 1969), 9-17; reprinted in S's Literary Dimensions: A Guide to Comparative Studies, ed. T. Hayashi, 1973. pp. 46-54.

769. _____. "Teaching S," A Study Guide to S: A Handbook to His Major Works, ed. T. Hayashi, 1974. pp. 1-4.

770. Lojek, Helen. "Jim Casey: Politico of the New Jerusalem," SQ, 15 (Winter-Spring 1982), 30-37 [The Grapes of Wrath].

771. Lutwack, Leonard. "The Grapes of Wrath as Heroic

Fiction," in his Heroic Fiction: The Epic Tradition
and American Novels of the 20th Century. Carbon-
dale: Southern Illinois University Press, 1971. pp.
47-63; reprinted in 20th Century Interpretations of
"The Grapes of Wrath," ed. R. C. Davis, 1982.
pp. 63-75.

772. McCarthy, Kevin M. "Witchcraft and Superstition in
The Winter of Our Discontent," New York Folklore
Q, 30 (September 1974), 197-211.

773. McCarthy, Paul. "House and Shelter as Symbol in The
Grapes of Wrath," South Dakota R, 5 (1967-1968),
48-67.

774. McConnell, Frank D. "Film and Writing: The Political Dimension," Massachusetts R, 13 (Autumn
1972), 543-62 [In Dubious Battle].

775. McDaniel, Barbara A. "Alienation in East of Eden:
'The Chart of the Soul,'" SQ, 14 (Winter-Spring
1981), 32-39.

775a. _____. "JS: Recent Publications," West Coast R,
12 (January 1978), 55-59.

776. MacKendrick, Louis K. "The Popular Art of Discontent: S's Masterful Winter," SQ, 12 (Summer-Fall
1979), 99-107.

777. McWilliams, Wilson Warren. "Natty Bumppo and The
Godfather," Colorado Q, 24 (Autumn 1975), 133-44
[S's Characters].

778. Magee, John D. "Painting of Cannery Row," SQ, 5
(Spring 1972), 59.

779. Magny, Claude Edmonde. "S, or The Limits of the
Impersonal Novel," in his The Age of the American
Novel, tr. Eleanor Hockman. New York: Ungar
Press, 1972. pp. 161-77.

780. Maloff, S. "S," New York Times Book R, October
26, 1975, pp. 5-6.

781. "Manuscripts III: Tortilla Flat by JS," Library Chronicle of the University of Texas, 3 (1971), 80-81.

782. Marks, Lester J. "East of Eden: 'Thou Mayest,'"
SQ, 4 (Winter 1971), 3-18 [Reprint of a chapter
from his Thematic Design in the Novels of JS. The
Hague: Mouton, 1969].

783. Marovitz, Sanford E. "The Cryptic Raillery of 'Saint
Katy the Virgin,'" SQ, 5 (Summer-Fall 1972), 107-
12; reprinted in A Study Guide to S's "The Long
Valley," ed. T. Hayashi, 1976. pp. 73-80.

784. _____. "The Expository Prose of JS," (Part I),
SQ, 7 (Spring 1974), 41-53; (Part II), 7 (Summer-
Fall 1974), 88-102.

785. _____. "JS and Adlai Stevenson: The Shattered
Image of America," S's Literary Dimensions: A
Guide to Comparative Studies, ed. T. Hayashi,
1973. pp. 116-29.

786. Martin, Arthur W. "Sex Life Among the Octopi: An
Example of the Esoteric Knowledge Shared by S and
Ricketts," S and the Sea, eds. R. Astro and J. W.
Hedgpeth, 1975. pp. 35-37.

787. Martin, Bruce K. "'The Leader of the People' Re-
examined," Studies in Short Fiction, 8 (Summer
1971), 423-32.

788. Matsumoto, Fusae. "S's Women in The Long Valley,"
JS: East and West (SMS, No. 8), ed. T. Hayashi,
et al., 1978. pp. 48-53.

789. Matton, Collin G. "Water Imagery and the Conclusion
to The Grapes of Wrath," NEMLA Newsletter, 2
(May 1970), 44-47.

790. Mawer, Randall. "Takeshi Kato, 'Good American':
The Central Episode in S's The Pastures of Heaven,"
SQ, 13 (Winter-Spring 1980), 23-31.

791. May, Charles E. "Myth and Mystery in S's 'The
Snake': A Jungian View," Criticism, 15 (Fall 1973),
322-35.

792. Meador, Roy. "JS: Born to Write," Air California
Magazine, 12 (April 1980), 47-49; 54; 56.

793. Mendelson, Maurice. "From The Grapes of Wrath to The Winter of Our Discontent," in 20th Century American Literature: A Soviet View, tr. Ronald Vroon. Moscow: Progress, 1976. pp. 411-26.

794. Metzger, Charles R. "The Film Version of S's The Pearl," SQ, 4 (Summer 1971), 88-92.

795. _____. "S's Cannery Row (1945)," A Study Guide to S: A Handbook to His Major Works, ed. T. Hayashi, 1974. pp. 19-28.

796. _____. "S's Mexican-Americans," S: The Man and His Work, eds. R. Astro and T. Hayashi, 1971. pp. 141-55.

797. _____. "S's The Pearl as a Non-teleological Parable of Hope," Research Studies, 46 (1978), 98-105.

798. Miller, William V. "Sexual and Spiritual Ambiguity in 'The Chrysanthemums'," SQ, 5 (Summer-Fall 1972), 68-75; reprinted in A Study Guide to S's "The Long Valley," ed. T. Hayashi, 1976. pp. 1-10.

799. Millichap, Joseph. "Realistic Style in S's and Milestone's Of Mice and Men," Literature/Film Q, 6 (Summer 1978), 241-52.

800. Mitchell, Marilyn L. "S's Strong Women: Feminine Identity in the Short Stories," Southwest R, 61 (Summer 1976), 304-15; reprinted in S's Women (SMS, No. 9), ed. T. Hayashi, 1979. pp. 26-35.

801. Mitchell, Robin C. "S and Malory: A Correspondence with Eugène Vinaver," SQ, 10 (Summer-Fall 1977), 70-79.

802. Momose, Fumio. "On The Pastures of Heaven: A Survey of Criticism," Hosei University General Education Q, 36 (February 1980), 107-17.

803. Monta, Shoji. "S's View of Womanhood: The Meaning of 'the time of waiting' in The Long Valley," Chu-Shikoku Studies in American Literature, 8 (March 1972), 39-52.

804. Morris, Harry. "The Pearl: Realism and Allegory,"

English Journal, 52 (October 1963), 487-95; 505; reprinted in S: A Collection of Critical Essays, ed. R. M. Davis, 1972. pp. 149-62.

805. Morsberger, Katherine M., and Robert E. Morsberger. "'The Murder': Realism or Ritual?" A Study Guide to S's "The Long Valley," ed. T. Hayashi, 1976. pp. 65-71.

806. Morsberger, Robert E. "Adrift in S's Lifeboat," Literature/Film Q, 4 (Fall 1976), 325-38; reprinted in Proceedings of the Fifth National Convention of the Popular Culture Association, ed. Michael Marsden, 1975. pp. 405-29.

807. _____. "In Defense of Westering ['The Leader of the People'], " WAL, 5 (Summer 1970), 133-46.

808. _____. "Of Mice, Dogs, Wabbits, Ducks, and Men," SQ, 14 (Summer-Fall 1981), 112.

809. _____. "The Price of 'The Harness, ' " SQ, 6 (Winter 1973), 24-27.

810. _____. "S on Screen," A Study Guide to S: A Handbook to His Major Works, ed. T. Hayashi, 1974. pp. 258-98.

811. _____. "S's Happy Hookers," SQ, 9 (Summer-Fall 1976), 101-15; reprinted in S's Women, (SMS, No. 9), ed. T. Hayashi, 1979. pp. 36-48.

812. _____. "S's Zapata: Rebel vs. Revolutionary, " S: The Man and His Work, eds. R. Astro and T. Hayashi, 1971. pp. 43-63; reprinted in JS's "Viva Zapata!," ed. R. E. Morsberger. New York: Viking Press, 1975. pp. xi-xxxviii.

813. _____. "S's Viva Zapata! (Screenplay, 1952; published 1975)," A Study Guide to S (Part II), ed. T. Hayashi, 1979. pp. 191-09.

814. _____. "S's The Wayward Bus (1947)," A Study Guide to S (Part II), ed. T. Hayashi, 1979. pp. 210-31.

815. Mortlock, Melanie. "The Eden Myth as Paradox: An

Allegorical Reading of The Pastures of Heaven,"
SQ, 11 (Winter 1978), 6-15.

816. Murray, Edward. "JS, Point of View, and Film,"
Cinematic Imagination. New York: Ungar Press,
1972. pp. 261-77.

817. Murray, Iseobel, and Jim Merriless. "East of Eden,"
New Blackfriars, 53 (March 1972), 130-35.

818. _____, and _____. "This Side of Paradise: Old
Testament Themes in JS's Fiction," New Blackfriars
(University of Leeds, England), 53 (February 1972),
60-68.

819. Nakashima, Saikichi. "S's Women," KAL, 17 (September 1976), 75-76.

820. Nakayama, Kiyoshi. "The Artist Design of The Grapes
of Wrath: S's Five Layers of Symbolism," Kansai
University Essays and Studies, 31 (March 1982),
117-25.

820a. _____. "On S's The Wayward Bus," Kansai University Literary Q, 25 (1975), 129-54.

821. _____. "An Oriental Interpretation of S's Literature
and Thought," JS: East and West (SMS, No. 8),
ed. T. Hayashi, et al., 1978. pp. 71-82.

822. _____. "S Criticism in Japan: 1976-1977," SQ, 12
(Summer-Fall 1979), 115-22.

823. _____. "S Criticism in Japan: 1978-1979," SQ, 14
(Summer-Fall 1981), 105-11.

824. Nimitz, Jack. "Ecology in The Grapes of Wrath,"
Hartford Studies in Literature, 2 (1970), 165-68.

825. Noverr, Douglas A. "The JS Issue: An Overview,"
American Examiner, 6 (Fall-Winter 1978-79), ed.
Douglas A. Noverr, 1-5.

826. O'Brien, Maureen. "JS's Fiction 1940-1950," Studies
in English Literature (Okayama, Japan), 9 (1974),
[n. p.].

827. O'Connor, Margaret Anne. See her reviews of S publications in American Literary Scholarship/An Annual, ed. James Woodress (1974-77). See also French, Warren (1971-73), and Salzman, Jack (1978-   ).

828. Ortega, Philip. "Fables of Identity: Stereotype and Caricature of Chicanos in S's Tortilla Flat," Journal of Ethnic Studies, 1 (1973), 39-43.

829. Osborne, William. "The Education of Elisa Allen: Another Reading of JS's 'The Chrysanthemums'," Interpretations, 8 (1976), 10-15.

830. _____. "The Texts of S's 'The Chrysanthemums'," Interpretations: Studies in Language and Literature, 9 (1977), 34-39.

831. Ousby, Ian. Reader's Guide to 50 American Novels. New York: Barnes and Noble, 1979. pp. 303-15.

832. Owens, Louis D. "JS's 'Mystical Outcrying': To a God Unknown and The Log from the Sea of Cortez," SJS, 5 (May 1979), 21-32.

833. _____. "S's 'Flight': Into the Jaws of Death," SQ 10 (Summer-Fall 1977), 103-08.

834. _____. "The Threshold of War: S's Quest in Once There Was a War," SQ, 13 (Summer-Fall 1980), 80-86.

835. _____. "The Wayward Bus: The Triumph of Nature," SJS, 6 (February 1980), 45-53.

836. Palmieri, Anthony F. R. "In Dubious Battle: A Portrait in Pessimism," RE: Artes Liberales, 3 (1976), 61-71.

837. Pearce, Howard D. "S's 'The Leader of the People': Dialectic and Symbol," Papers on Language and Literature 8 (Fall 1972), 415-26.

838. Perez, Betty L. "The Form of the Narrative Section of Sea of Cortez: A Specimen Collected from Reality," SQ, 9 (Spring 1976), 36-44; reprinted in S's Travel Literature (SMS, No. 10), ed. T. Hayashi, 1980. pp. 47-55.

839. _____ . "House and Home: Thematic Symbols in The Grapes of Wrath," JS: "The Grapes of Wrath": Text and Criticism, ed. P. Lisca, 1972. pp. 840-53.

840. _____ . "S, Ricketts, and Sea of Cortez: Partnership or Exploitation?" SQ, 7 (Summer-Fall 1974), 73-79.

841. _____ . "S's In Dubious Battle (1936)," A Study Guide to S: A Handbook to His Major Works, ed. T. Hayashi, 1974. pp. 47-68.

842. Peterson, Richard F. "The God in the Darkness: A Study of JS and D. H. Lawrence," S's Literary Dimension: A Guide to Comparative Studies, ed. T. Hayashi, 1973. pp. 67-82.

843. _____ . "The Grail Legend and S's 'The Great Mountains,'" SQ, 6 (Winter 1973), 9-15; reprinted in A Study Guide to S's "The Long Valley," ed. T. Hayashi, 1976. pp. 89-96.

844. _____ . "Homer Was Blind: JS on the Character of William Faulkner," SQ, 11 (Winter 1978), 15-20.

845. _____ . "Introduction" to S's Women (SMS, No. 9), ed. T. Hayashi, 1979. pp. viii-x.

846. _____ . "Mon Semblable, Mon Frère: Advice to the Young S Critic," SQ, 9 (Summer-Fall 1976), 88-91.

847. _____ . "The Mythology of American Life: America and Americans (1966)," A Study Guide to S: A Handbook to His Major Works, ed. T. Hayashi, 1974. pp. 5-18; reprinted in S's Travel Literature (SMS, No. 10), ed. T. Hayashi, 1980. pp. 11-21.

848. _____ . "S's East of Eden (1952)," A Study Guide to S (Part II), ed. T. Hayashi, 1979. pp. 63-86.

849. _____ . "S's The Log from the Sea of Cortez (1951)," A Study Guide to S (Part II), ed. T. Hayashi, 1979. pp. 87-99.

850. _____ . "The Turning Point: The Pastures of Heaven (1932)," A Study Guide to S: A Handbook to His Major Works, ed. T. Hayashi, 1974. pp. 87-106.

851. Piacentino, E. J. "Patterns of Animal Imagery in S's 'Flight,'" Studies in Short Fiction, 17 (Fall 1980), 437-43.

852. Pizer, Donald. "JS and American Naturalism," SQ, 9 (Winter 1976), 12-15.

853. Poulikidas, Andreas K. "S, Kazantzakis and Socialism," SQ, 3 (Summer 1970), 62-72; reprinted in S's Literary Dimensions: A Guide to Comparative Studies, ed. T. Hayashi, 1973. pp. 55-66; Actes du Vie: Congrès de l'Association Internationale de Literature, eds. Michel Cadot, et al., 1975. pp. 781-84.

854. Powell, Lawrence Clark. "JS: To a God Unknown," in his California Classics. Los Angeles: W. Ritchie Press, 1971. pp. 220-30.

855. "No entry."

856. Pratt, Linda Ray. "Imagining Existence: Form and History in S and Agee," Southern R, 11 (January 1975), 84-98 [The Grapes of Wrath].

857. _____. "In Defense of Mac's Dubious Battle," SQ, 10 (Spring 1977), 36-44.

858. Raess, John. "S Used San Jose Hangings for Short Story with Lynching Theme," Spartan Daily (San Jose State University), April 26, 1978. 1, 8.

859. Rao, V. Ramachandra. "S," The American Fictional Hero (Series in English Language and Literature, IV). Bahri, India: Chandigarh, 1979 [n. p.].

860. Reed, John R. "The Grapes of Wrath and the Esthetics of Indigence," JS: "The Grapes of Wrath": Text and Criticism, ed. P. Lisca, 1972. pp. 825-39.

861. Reitt, B. B. "I Never Returned as I Went In: S's Travels with Charley," Southwest R, 66 (Spring 1981), 186-200.

862. Riggs, Susan F. "S at Stanford," Stanford Magazine, 4 (Fall/Winter 1976), 14-21.

863. Robbins, Robert J. "Additional Comments on 'S and de Maupassant: A Parallel Occurrence,'" SQ, 13 (Summer-Fall 1980), 86.

864. Rose, Alan Henry. "S and the Complexity of the Self in In Dubious Battle," SQ, 9 (Winter 1976), 15-19.

865. Rosenstone, Robert A. "S's America: Myth and Reality," KAL, 17 (September 1976), 85-86.

866. Rousseau, Richard W. "Secular and Christian Images of Man," Thought, 47 (Summer 1972), 165-200 [S, Koestler, Eliot, Bernanos, Sartre, and Camus].

867. Sabchack, V. C. "The Grapes of Wrath: Thematic Emphasis Through Visual Style," American Q, 31 (Winter 1979), 596-615 [Adaptation].

868. Salter, Christopher L. "JS's The Grapes of Wrath as a Primer for Cultural Geography," Humanistic Geography and Literature: Essays on the Experience of Place, ed. Douglas C. D. Pocock. London: Croom Helm, 1981. pp. 142-58.

869. Salzman, Jack. See his annual reviews of S publications in American Literary Scholarship/An Annual, ed. James Woodress (1978-). See also French, Warren (1971-73), and O'Connor, Margaret Anne (1974-77).

870. Sarchett, Barry W. "In Dubious Battle: A Reevaluation," SQ, 13 (Summer-Fall 1980), 87-97.

871. Sastry, P. S. "The Structure of The Grapes of Wrath," Indian Journal of English Studies, 1 (1971) [n. p.].

872. Satyanarayana, M. R. "'And Then the Child Becomes a Man': Three Initiation Stories of JS," Indian Journal in American Studies, 1 (November 1971), 87-93 [The Red Pony, "Flight," and The Raid].

873. _____. "From Winesburg to Salinas in Search of Love," Osmania Journal of English Studies, 8 (1971), 19-28 [Sherwood Anderson's Winesburg, Ohio and S's The Long Valley].

874. _____. "JS's Unknown God," Indian Journal in American Studies, 3 (June 1973), 1-7.

875. Schamberger, J. Edward. "Grapes of Gladness: A Misconception of Walden," American Transcendental Q, 13 (Winter 1972), 15-16 [The Grapes of Wrath].

876. Scheer, Ronald. Of Mice and Men: Novel, Play, Movie," American Examiner, ed. Douglas A. Noverr, 6 (Fall-Winter 1978-79), 6-39.

877. Scott, Roger. "Henry Fonda, Maureen O'Hara to Film The Red Pony," Daily Union Democrat (Sonora, Cal.), August 16, 1972 [n. p.].

878. _____. "The Red Pony: Henry Fonda Comes to Tuolumne's Hills," Daily Union Democrat, August 2, 1972 [n. p.].

879. Seet, Charles A., Jr. "Ms. Elisa Allen and S's 'The Chrysanthemums,'" MFS, 20 (Summer 1974), 210-14.

880. Shastri, P. S. "The Structure of The Grapes of Wrath," Indian Journal of English Studies, 12 (December 1971), 67-74.

881. Shepherd, Allen. "On the Dubiousness of S's In Dubious Battle," Notes on Modern American Literature, 2 (1978), Item 19.

882. Shimada, Saburo. "Plant Description in Willa Cather and JS's Literary Works (I), (II)," Kemmei Women's Junior College Bulletin, 14 (1979), 1-46; 15 (1980), 1-47.

883. Shimomura, Noboru. "Christianity and Eastern Philosophy in East of Eden," Kure Technical College Report (Japan), 13 (March 1977), 1-46.

884. _____. "Guilt and Christianity in The Pearl," Chu-Shikoku Studies in American Literature, 16 (1980) [n. p.].

884a. _____. "Hemingway and S: Their Respective Religious Perception," Studies in English and American Literature and Language in Commemoration of Professor Hiroshige Yoshida's Retirement. Tokyo: Shinozaki Shorin, 1980. pp. 498-507.

885. _____ . "Humor and Mysticism in Tortilla Flat," Shimane University Law and Letters College Q, 3 (December 1980), 143-70.

886. _____ . "Mysticism in JS's Novels," JS: East and West (SMS, No. 8), eds. T. Hayashi, et al., 1978. pp. 83-90.

887. _____ . "Mysticism in To a God Unknown," Kure Technical College Q, 9 (February 1974), 9-26.

888. _____ . "Social Concern and Mysticism in The Grapes of Wrath," Kure Technical College Q, 12 (October 1976), 9-26.

889. Shively, Charles. "JS: From the Tide Pool to the Loyal Community," S: The Man and His Work, eds. R. Astro and T. Hayashi, 1971. pp. 25-34.

890. Short, John D., Jr. "JS: A 1930s Photo-Recollection," SJS, 2 (May 1976), 74-82.

891. Short, M. H. "A Stylistic Analysis of JS's Of Mice and Men," M. A. Thesis, University of Birmingham, England, 1970, SQ, 5 (Spring 1972), 58 (abstract].

892. Shurgot, Michael W. "A Game of Cards in S's Of Mice and Men," SQ, 15 (Winter-Spring 1982), 38-43.

893. Simmonds, Roy S. "The First Publication of S's 'The Leader of the People,'" SQ, 8 (Winter 1975), 13-18.

894. _____ . "JS, Robert Louis Stevenson, and Edith McGillcuddy," SJS, 1 (November 1975), 29-39.

895. _____ . "A Note on S's Unpublished Arthurian Stories," S and the Arthurian Theme (SMS, No. 5), ed. T. Hayashi, 1975. pp. 25-29.

896. _____ . "The Original Manuscripts of S's 'The Chrysanthemums,'" SQ, 7 (Summer-Fall 1974), 102-11.

897. _____ . "'Our land ... incredibly dear and beautiful': S's America and Americans," SQ, 8 (Summer-Fall 1975), 89-95; reprinted as "S's America and

Americans, " in S's Travel Literature (SMS, No. 10), ed. T. Hayashi, 1980. pp. 21-27.

898. _____. "S's 'The Murder': A Critical and Bibliographical Study, " SQ, 9 (Spring 1976), 45-53.

899. _____. "S's Sweet Thursday (1954), " A Study Guide to S (Part II), ed. T. Hayashi, 1979. pp. 139-64.

900. _____. "S's Travels with Charley (1962), " A Study Guide to S (Part II), ed. T. Hayashi, 1979. pp. 165-90.

901. _____. "The Unrealized Dream: S's Modern Version of Malory, " S and the Arthurian Theme (SMS, No. 5), ed. T. Hayashi, 1975. pp. 30-43.

902. Simpson, Arthur L. , Jr. "S's Tortilla Flat (1935), " A Study Guide to His Major Works, ed. T. Hayashi, 1974. pp. 214-43.

903. _____. " 'The White Quail': A Portrait of an Artist, " SQ, 5 (Summer-Fall 1972), 76-80; reprinted in A Study Guide to S's "The Long Valley, " ed. T. Hayashi, 1976. pp. 11-16.

904. "No entry. "

905. Slade, Leonard A. , Jr. "The Use of Biblical Allusion in The Grapes of Wrath, " CLA Journal, 11 (March 1968), 241-47.

906. Slater, John F. "American Past and Soviet Present: The Double Consciousness of S's A Russian Journal, " SQ, 8 (Summer-Fall 1975), 95-104.

907. _____. "S's Of Mice and Men (Novel) (1937), " A Study Guide to S: A Handbook to His Major Works, " ed. T. Hayashi, 1974. pp. 129-54.

908. "No entry. "

909. Spies, George H. , III. "The Dramatic Structure of JS's Of Mice and Men, " KAL, 13 (December 1971), 60-65.

910. _____. "JS's In Dubious Battle and Robert Penn

Warren's Night Rider: A Comparative Study," S's
Literary Dimension: A Guide to Comparative Studies,
ed. T. Hayashi, 1973. pp. 130-37.

911. _____. "S and the Automobile," SQ, 7 (Winter
1974), 18-24.

912. Spilka, Mark. "Of George and Lennie and Curley's
Wife: Sweet Violence in S's Eden," MFS, 20 (Summer 1974), 169-79.

913. Steele, Joan. "A Century of Idiots: Barnaby Rudge
and Of Mice and Men," 5 (Winter 1972), 8-17; reprinted in S's Literary Dimension: A Guide to Comparative Studies, ed. T. Hayashi, 1973. pp. 16-
27.

914. Stein, Joseph A. "S Learned About Life in the Tidal
Pools," Portland Oregonian (Sunday Supplement).
July 14, 1974. pp. 4-5.

915. Stoddard, Shirlie. "Fires on the Bay: Will Cannery
Row Survive?" Coast Magazine [n. v.] (July 1973),
37-43.

916. Stone, Donal. "S, Jung, and The Winter of Our Discontent," SQ, 11 (Summer-Fall 1978), 87-96.

917. Street, Webster. "JS: A Reminiscence," S: The
Man and His Work, eds. R. Astro and T. Hayashi,
1971. pp. 35-41.

918. _____. "Remembering JS," SJS, 1 (November 1975),
109-27.

919. Strout, Cushing. "Radical Religion and the American
Political Novel," The Veracious Imagination by C.
Strout. Middletown, Conn.: Wesleyan University
Press, 1980. pp. 70-91.

920. Sugiyama, Takahiko. "S Criticism: Present and Fu-
ture," JS: East and West (SMS, No. 8), eds. T.
Hayashi, et al., 1978. pp. 1-6.

921. Sullivan, E. W., II. "Cur in 'The Chrysanthemums,'"
Studies in Short Fiction, 16 (Summer 1979), 215-17.

922. "No entry."

923. Swan, Kenneth D. "JS: In Search of America," S's
Prophetic Vision of America, eds. T. Hayashi and
K. D. Swan, 1976. pp. 12-27.

924. _____. "The Merit of JS: A Wide-Ranging Debate,"
S's Prophetic Vision of America, eds. T. Hayashi
and K. D. Swan, 1976. pp. 56-84.

925. Sweet, Charles. "Ms. Elisa Allen and S's 'The Chrysanthemums,'" MFS, 20 (Summer 1974), 210-14.

926. Tarp, Fred. "JS: Some Reflections," S and the Sea,
eds. R. Astro and J. W. Hedgpeth, 1975. pp. 29-
33.

927. Taylor, Walter Fuller. "The Grapes of Wrath Recon-
sidered," Mississippi Q, 12 (Summer 1959), 139-
44; reprinted in JS: "The Grapes of Wrath": Text
and Criticism, ed. P. Lisca, 1972. pp. 757-68.

928. Teichmann, Howard. "S," George S. Kauffman: An
Intimate Portrait. New York: Atheneum, 1972.
pp. 148-51.

929. Tokunaga, Masanori. "The Biological Descriptions in
The Pearl and Their Meanings," KAL, 16 (September 1977), 13-16.

930. _____. "A Return to Nature--S's Search for American Civilization," KAL, 17 (September 1976), 20-24.

931. Tokunaga, Toshiaki. "JS's Travels with Charley,"
KAL, 15 (May 1974), 46-53.

932. Toshido, Tsutsumi. "Sea of Cortez: S and Ecology,"
Journal of Obirin University and Junior College, 13
(April 1973), [n. d.].

933. Trachtenberg, Stanley. "JS: The Fate of Protest,"
North Dakota Q, 41 (Spring 1973), 5-11.

934. _____. "West's Locust: Laughing at the Laugh,"
Michigan Q R, 14 (1975), 187-98 [Nathanael West's
Day of The Locust and S's The Grapes of Wrath].

935. Tsuboi, Kiyohiko. "S's Cup of Gold and Fitzgerald's
The Great Gatsby," JS: East and West (SMS, No.
8), ed. T. Hayashi, et al., 1978. pp. 40-47.

936. "No entry."

937. Vassilowitch, John, Jr. "Bing Crosby and The Grapes of Wrath: Bad History, Good Art," SQ, 13 (Summer-Fall 1980), 97-98.

938. Verdier, Douglas L. "Ethan Allen Hawley and the Hanged Man: Free Will and Fate in The Winter of Our Discontent," SQ, 15 (Winter-Spring 1982), 44-50.

939. Walcutt, Charles Child (comp.). "S," Seven Novelists in the American Naturalist Tradition: An Introduction. Minneapolis: University of Minnesota Press, 1974. pp. 205-44.

940. Waldron, Edward E. "The Pearl and The Old Man and the Sea: A Comparative Analysis," SQ, 13 (Summer-Fall 1980), 98-106.

941. Watkins, Floyd C. "Flat Wine from The Grapes of Wrath," The Humanist in His World: Essays in Honor of Fielding, eds. Barbara Bitter and Frederick Sanders. Greenwood, S. C.: Attic, 1976. pp. 57-69.

942. West, Philip J. "S's 'The Leader of the People': A Crisis in Style," WAL, 5 (Summer 1970). pp. 137-41.

943. White, Ray Lewis. "Sherwood Anderson Meets JS: 1939," SQ, 11 (Winter 1978), 20-22.

944. _____. "S and de Maupassant: A Parallel Occurrence," SQ, 12 (Winter-Spring 1979), 27-29.

945. Whitman, Alden. "JS," The Obituary Book. New York: Stein and Day, 1971. pp. 176-83.

946. Williams, William Appleman. "S and the Spirit of the Thirties," S and the Sea, eds. R. Astro and J. W. Hedgpeth, 1975. pp. 39-44.

947. Wilson, Jerry W. "In Dubious Battle: Engagement in Collectivity," SQ, 13 (Winter-Spring 1980), 31-42.

948. Wood, Marylaird. "Because a City Cared: S House

Saved," Christian Science Monitor. Friday, May 3, 1974. FS.

949. Woodward, Robert H. "JS, Edith McGillcuddy, and Tortilla Flat: A Problem in Manuscript Dating," SJS, 3 (November 1977), 70-73.

950. _____. "Postal Stamp to Honor Author S," Collector, 9 (February 1979), 3-5.

951. _____. "The Promise of S's 'The Promise'," SQ, 6 (Winter 1973), 15-19; reprinted in A Study Guide to S's "The Long Valley," ed. T. Hayashi, 1976. pp. 97-103.

952. Work, Robert E. "Editorially Speaking: So They Don't Like S," SJS, 1 (November 1975), 102.

953. _____. "S and the Spartan Daily," SJS, 1 (November 1975), 103-07.

954. Wright, Thomas L. "S's The Acts of King Arthur and His Noble Knights from the Winchester Manuscripts of Thomas Malory and Other Sources," Southern Humanities R, 13 (Summer 1979), 173-74.

955. Wyatt, Bryant N. "Experimentation in Technique: The Protest Novels of JS," Discourse, 12 (Spring 1969), 143-53 [In Dubious Battle, Of Mice and Men, and The Grapes of Wrath].

956. Yamamoto, Shuji. "Tortilla Flat: Value System Examined," Kurume University Journal, 1 (June 1975) [n. p.].

957. Yano, Shigeharu. "An Analysis of Sin in The Winter of Our Discontent," Bulletin of Reitaku University, 30 (December 1980), 55-70.

957a. _____. "Dreams and Realities in America and Americans," Bulletin of Reitaku University, 21 (July 1976), 1-33.

958. _____. "The Grapes of Wrath: The Symbol of Eternity," Bulletin of Reitaku University, 23 (July 1977), 35-57.

959. _____. "Humanity in The Short Reign of Pippin IV," Bulletin of Reitaku University, 24 (December 1977), 17-38.

960. _____. "The Imagery in The Winter of Our Discontent," Bulletin of Reitaku University, 12 (August 1971), 116-39.

961. _____. "Life and Death in The Red Pony," Bulletin of Reitaku University, 16 (November 1973), 1-20.

962. _____. "Love and Death in Of Mice and Men," Bulletin of Reitaku University, 24 (December 1977), 39-58.

963. _____. "Man, Society and Nature in Travels with Charley," Bulletin of Reitaku University, 20 (December 1975), 15-42.

964. _____. "A Mechanism of Defense in In Dubious Battle (I) (II)," Bulletin of Reitaku University, 27 (July 1979), 69-85; 28 (December 1979), 1-16.

965. _____. "Psychological Description in The Wayward Bus," Bulletin of Reitaku University, 13 (March 1972), 1-19.

966. _____. "Psychological Interpretation of S's Women in The Long Valley," JS: East and West (SMS, No. 8), ed. T. Hayashi, et al., 1978. pp. 54-60.

967. _____. "The Relation Between Fortune and Freedom in Tortilla Flat," Bulletin of Reitaku University, 15 (March 1973), 41-63.

968. _____. "Right and Wrong in The Moon Is Down," Bulletin of Reitaku University, 11 (January 1971), 15-32.

969. _____. "The Three Worlds in The Long Valley (1) (2) (3)," Bulletin of Reitaku University, 17 (June 1974), 1-15; 18 (February 1975), 1-18; 19 (July 1975), 63-81.

970. _____. "Timshel in East of Eden," Bulletin of Reitaku University, 14 (December 1972), 55-70.

971. Yarmus, Marcia D. "JS and the Hispanic Influence," SQ, 10 (Summer-Fall 1977), 97-102.

972. Yokozawa, Kyoko. "The Pearl: Techniques and Imagery," Bulletin of the Faculty of Liberal Arts, 3 (May 1977), [n. p.].

973. Yoshizawa, Eijiro. "On The Grapes of Wrath by JS," Kumazawa University Foreign Language Bulletin (Tokyo, Japan), 12 (1980), 103-17.

974. Yoshizu, Shigeharu. "Emerson and S--On the Oriental Concept of Being," Studies in English Literature, 10 (November 1974), [n. p.].

975. Zollman, Sol. "JS's Political Outlook in The Grapes of Wrath," Literature and Ideology (Canada), 13 (1972), 9-20.

K. REVIEWS (A Selected Checklist of Reviews of Primary and Secondary Works Including Books, Theater, TV, Film, and Opera Reviews)

N. B.: (1) French, Warren (1971-73); O'Connor, Margaret Anne (1974-77); Salzman, Jack (1978-82): See their excellent reviews of S. criticism in American Literary Scholarship/ An Annual. Durham, N. C.: (Duke University Press).

N. B.: (2) A Collection of Reviews: See S. Criticism: A Review of Book-Length Studies (1939-1973) (SMS, No. 4), ed. T. Hayashi, 1974.

976. Allen, Robert V. (tr.). Russian Studies of American Literature: A Bibliography (1969).

   a) Keller, Dean H. SQ, 5 (Spring 1972), 51-52.

977. Allen, Walter. The Modern Novel in Britain and the United States (1964).

   a) Hamby, James A. SQ, 6 (Winter 1973), 27-29.

978. Astro, Richard. Edward F. Ricketts (1976).

    a) McDaniel, Barbara Albrecht. SQ, 12 (Winter-
    Spring 1979), 53-54.

979. _____. JS and Edward F. Ricketts (1973).

    a) Benton, Robert M. SQ, 8 (Winter 1975), 22-24.

    b) Ditsky, John. WAL, 9 (May 1974), 68-69.

    c) Hayashi, Tetsumaro. MFS, 20 (Winter 1974-
    75), 575-76.

    d) Willingham, J. R. Library Journal, 98 (Novem-
    ber 1, 1973), 3267.

980. _____, and Tetsumaro Hayashi (eds.). S. : The
Man and His Work (1971).

    a) Barbour, Brian M. SQ, 5 (Winter 1972), 19-
    22; reprinted in S. Criticism (SMS, No. 4), ed.
    T. Hayashi, 1974. pp. 28-30.

    b) French, Warren. "Reflections Prompted by
    Mr. Barbour's Review, " SQ, 5 (Summer-Fall
    1972), 118-20.

    c) Mitchell, Robin C. SQ, 11 (Summer-Fall 1978),
    109-12.

981. _____, and Joel W. Hedgpeth (eds.). S and the Sea
(1975).

    a) Beyer, Preston. SQ, 9 (Summer-Fall 1976),
    115-17.

982. Beach, Joseph Warren. American Fiction: 1920-1940
(1941).

    a) Hozeski, Bruce W. SQ, 5 (Spring 1972), 49-51.

983. Blake, Nelson Manfred. Novelists' America: Fiction
as History, 1910-1940 (1969).

    a) Knighton, Robert T. SQ, 6 (Spring 1973), 59-61.

984. Bluefarb, Sam. The Escape Motif in the American
Novel (1972).

　　　　a) Hoilman, Dennis R. SQ, 7 (Spring 1974), 53-55.

985. Bowden, Edwin T. The Dungeon of the Heart (1961).

　　　　a) MacDougall, James K. SQ, 7 (Summer-Fall 1974), 117.

986. Bradford Morrow Bookseller. JS: A Collection of Books and Manuscripts (1980).

　　　　a) Moore, Thomas J. SQ, 15 (Winter-Spring 1982), 58-60.

987. Bryer, Jackson R. Sixteen Modern American Authors (1974).

　　　　a) Mammola, Joseph L. SQ, 7 (Summer-Fall 1974), 119-20.

988. Burrows, Michael. JS and His Films (1970).

　　　　a) French, Warren. SQ, 6 (Spring 1973), 56.

　　　　b) Spies, George H., III. SQ, 6 (Summer 1973), 88-89.

989. Cook, Sylvia Jenkins. From Tobacco Road to Route 66 (1976).

　　　　a) Spies, George H., III. SQ, 10 (Summer-Fall 1977), 109-10.

990. Covici, Pascal, Jr. (ed.). The Portable S (1971).

　　　　a) Ditsky, John. SQ, 6 (Spring 1973), 54-56.

991. Cox, Martha H., and Robert H. Woodward (eds.). SJS (S Issue) (1975).

　　　　a) Slater, John F. SQ, 10 (Winter 1977), 22-29.

992. Crouch, Steve. S Country (1973).

　　　　a) Astro, Richard. WAL, 9 (August 1974), 144-45.

　　　　b) Morsberger, Robert E. SQ, 7 (Summer-Fall 1974), 120-22.

993. Davis, Robert Murray (ed.). S: A Collection of Critical Essays (1972).

    a) Ditsky, John. SMS, No. 4, ed. T. Hayashi, 1974. pp. 30-32.

994. Deakin, Motley, and Peter Lisca (eds.). From Irving to S (1972).

    a) Hoilman, Dennis H. SQ, 7 (Summer-Fall 1974), 114-15.

995. Ditsky, John. Essays on "East of Eden" (SMS, No. 7, 1977).

    a) Cohen, Sandy. Southern Humanities R, 13 (Summer 1979), 273-74.

    b) Woodward, Robert H. SQ, 11 (Summer-Fall 1978), 121-24.

996. Fensch, Thomas. S and Covici: The Story of a Friendship (1979).

    a) Chamberlain, J. New York Times (December 16, 1979) p. 17.

    b) Cohen, George. Chicago Tribune Book World, August 19, 1979. VII, 1.

    c) DeMott, Robert. JML, 8 (Nos. 3-4, 1981), 617-19.

    d) Govoni, Mark W. SQ, 13 (Summer-Fall 1980), 109-10.

    e) Kirsch, Robert. Los Angeles Times, August 24, 1979. IV, 7.

    f) Lehmann-Haupt, C. New York Times, August 31, 1979. C20.

    g) Morsberger, Robert E. WAL, 15 (Summer 1980), 154-55.

997. Floyd, Carlisle. Of Mice and Men, opera after JS's play-novel (1980).

    a) Ditsky, John. SQ, 14 (Summer-Fall 1981), 130-31.

998. French, Warren. The Fifties: Fiction, Poetry, Drama (1970).

    a) Trimmer, Joseph. SQ, 7 (Winter 1974), 27-28.

999. _____. Filmguide to "The Grapes of Wrath" (1973).

    a) Morsberger, Robert E. S Criticism (SMS, No. 4), ed. T. Hayashi, 1974. pp. 34-37.

1000. _____. JS (1975).

    a) Swan, Kenneth D. SQ, 9 (Spring 1976), 54-55.

1001. _____ (ed.). The Twenties: Fiction, Poetry, Drama (1975).

    a) Spies, George H., III. SQ, 10 (Summer-Fall 1977), 119-20.

1002. _____, and Walter Kidd (eds.). American Winners of the Nobel Literary Prize (1968).

    a) Peterson, Richard. SQ, 2 (Fall 1969), 61-63.

1003. Gale, Robert L. Barron's Simplified Approach to "The Grapes of Wrath" (1967).

    a) Siefker, Donald L. SQ, 7 (Winter 1974), 27.

1004. Garcia, Reloy. S and D. H. Lawrence: Fictive Voices and the Ethical Imperative (SMS, No. 2, 1972).

    a) Peterson, Richard F. SQ, 8 (Winter 1975), 29-31.

1005. Goldstone, Adrian H., and John R. Pagne. JS: A Bibliographical Catalogue of the Adrian H. Goldstone Collection (1974).

    a) Keller, Dean H. SQ, 8 (Summer-Fall 1975), 109-10, reprinted in A Handbook for S Collectors, Librarians, and Scholars (SMS, No. 11), ed. T. Hayashi, 1981. pp. 50-51.

1006. Gray, James. JS (1971).

a) Benson, Jackson J. SQ, 6 (Summer 1973), 80-84; 8 (Fall 1975), 110-12.

b) Fontenrose, Joseph. SQ, 8 (Winter 1975), 19-22.

1007.   Gross, John, and Lee Richard Hayman (eds.).   JS: A Guide to the Collection of the Salinas Public Library (1979).

a) Curcy, D. Steven.   Quarterly Newsletter of the Book Club of California, June 1979.   pp. 80-81.

b) Keller, Dean H.   SQ, 13 (Winter-Spring 1980) 46-47; reprinted in A Handbook for S Collectors, Librarians, and Scholars (SMS, No. 11), ed. T. Hayashi, 1981.   pp. 52-53.

1008.   Hakutani, Yoshinobu, and Lewis Fried (eds.).   American Literary Naturalism (1975).

a) Swan, Kenneth D.   SQ, 11 (Winter 1978), 24-27.

1009.   Harmon, Robert B.   The First Editions of JS (1978).

a) Smith, Juanita J.   SQ, 15 (Winter-Spring 1982), 61-62.

1010.   _____.   JS: Toward a Bibliography of Bibliographies (1973).

a) Keller, Dean H.   SQ, 7 (Summer-Fall 1974), 115-16.

1011.   Hashiguchi, Yasuo (ed.).   Short Stories by JS (1980).

a) Hamaguchi, Osamu.   SQ, 14 (Summer-Fall 1981), 117-18.

1012.   Hayashi, Tetsumaro (ed.).   JS: A Dictionary of His Fictional Characters (1976).

a) Tokunaga, Masanori.   KAL, 8 (October 1977), 66-67.

b) Woodward, Robert H.   SQ, 10 (Summer-Fall 1977), 112-14.

1013.   _____.   JS: A Guide to the Doctoral Dissertations (SMS, No. 1, 1971).

a) Seelhammer, Ruth. SQ, 6 (Fall 1973), 121-23.

1014. _____. A New Steinbeck Bibliography, 1929-1971
(1973).

a) Barbour, Brian M. S Criticism (SMS, No. 4),
ed. T. Hayashi, 1974. pp. 37-40; A Handbook
for S. Collectors, Librarians, and Scholars (SMS,
No. 11), ed. T. Hayashi, 1981. pp. 47-49.

b) Tsunematsu, Masao. Chu-Shikoku Studies in
American Literature 10 (January 1974), 49-52.

1015. _____ (ed.). S and Hemingway: Dissertation Abstracts and Research Opportunities (1980).

a) Dunbar, Maurice. SQ, 14 (Summer-Fall 1981),
113.

1016. _____. S Criticism: A Review of Book-Length
Studies (1929-1973) (SMS, No. 4, 1974).

a) Cox, Martha Heasley. SQ, 8 (Winter 1975), 24-
28.

b) Peterson, Richard F. SQ, 8 (Summer-Fall
1975), 116-19.

1017. _____ (ed.). S: The Arthurian Theme (SMS, No.
5, 1975).

a) Marovitz, Sanford E. SQ, 9 (Summer-Fall 1976),
118-20.

1018. _____ (ed.). S's Literary Dimension (1973).

a) Simmonds, Roy S. (SMS, No. 4), ed. T. Hayashi, 1974, pp. 40-44.

1019. _____ (ed.). S's Women (SMS, No. 9, 1979).

a) Hensley, Dennis E. Pacific Historian, 23 (Winter 1979), 116-17.

b) Hensley, Dennis E. SQ, 13 (Summer-Fall 1980),
115-17.

1020. _____ (ed.). A Study Guide to S: A Handbook to
His Major Works (1974).

a) LaFrance, Marston. SQ, 9 (Winter 1976), 27-28.

1021. _____ (ed.). A Study Guide to S (II) (1979).

a) DeMott, Robert. SQ, 15 (Winter-Spring 1982), 51-56.

b) Hamaguchi, Osamu. Chu-Shikoku Studies in American Literature, 17 (March 1981), 51-57.

1022. _____ (ed.). A Study Guide to S's "The Long Valley" (1976).

a) Gertzman, J. A. Studies in Short Fiction, 15 (Summer 1978), 337.

b) Matsumoto, Fusae. KAL, 19 (May 1978), 84-85.

c) Warner, Ronald C. SQ, 11 (Summer-Fall 1978), 119-21.

1023. _____, Yasuo Hashiguchi, and Richard F. Peterson (eds.). JS: East and West (SMS, No. 8, 1978).

a) DeMott, Robert. SJS, 6 (February 1980), 55-58.

b) McDaniel, Barbara Albrecht. SQ, 12 (Summer-Fall 1979), 123-25.

1024. _____, and Donald L. Siefker. The Special S Collection of the Ball State University Library: A Bibliographical Handbook (1972).

a) Keller, Dean H. SQ, 7 (Summer-Fall 1974), 116-17.

1025. _____, and Kenneth D. Swan (eds.). S's Prophetic Vision of America (1976).

a) Owens, Louis D. SQ, 11 (Summer-Fall 1978), 116-17.

1026. Hedgpeth, Joel W. (ed.). The Outer Shores: Ed Ricketts and JS Explore the Pacific Coast (Part I) (1978) and The Outer Shores: Breaking Through (Part II) (1979).

a) Moore, Thomas J. and Kenneth D. Swan. SQ, 14 (Summer-Fall 1981), 120-23.

1027. Jones, Lawrence W. JS as Fabulist, ed. Marston
LaFrance (SMS, No. 3, 1973).

   a) Spies, George H. , III. SQ, 8 (Summer-Fall
   1975), 114-16.

1028. Kiernan, Thomas. The Intricate Music: A Biography
of JS (1979).

   a) Aldridge, John W. New York Times Book Review, September 20, 1979. pp. 12, 22.

   b) Atkinson, David W. Lethebridge Herald: Books
   in Review (Canada), January 26, 1980. C:6.

   c) Brunette, Peter. Books and Arts, October 12,
   1979. pp. 16-17.

   d) DeMott, Robert. JML, 8 (Nos. 3-4, 1981), 617-
   19.

   e) Dunbar, Maurice. SQ, 13 (Summer-Fall 1980),
   107-09.

   f) Fensch, Thomas. Chicago Sun Times, September 2, 1979. p. 10.

   g) Galbraith, John Kenneth. New Republic, 181
   (August 25, 1979), 33-34.

   h) Rovit, Earl. Library Journal, 104 (September
   1, 1979), 1699.

   i) Skow, John. Time, 114 (October 1, 1979), 90.

   j) Wagenknecht, Edward. Chicago Tribune Book
   World, August 19, 1979. VII, 1.

1029. Knox, Maxine, and Mary Rodriguez. S's Street: Cannery Row (1980).

   a) Hayman, Lee Richard. SQ, 14 (Summer-Fall
   1981), 118-20.

1030. Levant, Howard. The Novels of JS: A Critical Study
(1974).

   a) Astro, Richard. SQ, 9 (Winter 1976), 24-27.

   b) DeMott, Robert. MFS, 21 (Winter 1975-76), 652-
   53.

   c) Fontenrose, Joseph. SJS, 1 (Nov. 1975) 139-41.

d) Isaacson, David. Library Journal, 100 (January 15, 1975), 130.

e) Lisca, Peter. AL, 47 (November 1975), 478.

1031. Lewis, Merrill, and L. L. Lee (eds.). The Westering Experience in American Literature (1977).

a) Owens, Louis D. SQ, 12 (Winter-Spring 1979), 55-57.

1032. "No entry."

1033. Lisca, Peter (ed.). JS: "The Grapes of Wrath": Text and Criticism (1972).

a) Simmonds, Roy S. S Criticism (SMS, No. 4), ed. T. Hayashi, 1974. pp. 32-34.

1034. _____. JS: Nature and Myth (1978).

a) Donohue, Agnes McNeill. AL, 50 (January 1979), 665-66.

b) Elswit, Sharon. School Library Journal, 24 (April 1978), 95.

c) McInerney, J. M. Best Sellers, 38 (October 1978), 231.

d) Peterson, Richard F. SQ, 12 (Winter-Spring 1979), 57-59.

1035. Lutwack, Leonard. Heroic Fiction: The Epic Tradition and American Novels of the Twentieth Century (1971).

a) Gadziola, David S. SQ, 7 (Summer-Fall 1974), 112-13.

1036. McCarthy, Paul. JS (1980).

a) Fensch, Thomas. SQ, 14 (Summer-Fall 1981), 114-15.

1037. Madden, Charles F. (ed.). Talks with Authors (1968).

a) Tenner, Robert L. SQ, 5 (Summer-Fall 1972), 113-14.

1038. Marks, Lester Jay. Thematic Design in the Novels
of JS (1969).

    a) Griffith, Malcolm. MFS, 4 (Fall 1971), 110-12.

1039. Messner, Mike. S Country in Dubious Homage (1979).

    a) Plummer, Linda. SQ, 13 (Summer-Fall 1980),
117-19.

1040. Milton, John R. The Novel of the American West
(1980).

    a) Tammaro, Thomas M. SQ, 15 (Winter-Spring
1982), 62-63.

1041. Nabeshima, Yoshihiro, and Mikio Inui (trs.). Cup of
Gold (1979).

    a) Momose, Fumio. SQ, 13 (Winter-Spring 1980),
51-53.

1042. Nobel Foundation and The Swedish Academy. Nobel
Prize Library: Faulkner/O'Neill/Steinbeck (1971).

    a) Woodward, Robert H. SQ, 7 (Summer-Fall
1974), 122-24.

1043. Noverr, Douglas A. (ed.). The American Examiner
(Special S Issue) (1978-1979).

    a) Wilson, Jerry W. SQ, 14 (Summer-Fall 1981),
125-27.

1044. Okamoto, Hideo, and Michio Kato (eds.). Three
Stories from "The Long Valley" (1974).

    a) Yano, Shigeharu. SQ, 10 (Summer-Fall 1977),
114-15.

1045. Otake, Masaru, and Yukio Rizawa (eds.). A Study of
JS (1980).

    a) Hamaguchi, Osamu. SQ, 15 (Winter-Spring
1982), 56-57.

1046. Panichas, George A. (ed.). The Politics of 20th Century Novelists (1971).

a) MacDougall, James K. SQ, 7 (Summer-Fall 1974), 118.

1047. Perkins, George (ed.). The Theory of the American Novel (1970).

a) MacDougall, James K. SQ, 6 (Winter 1973), 29-31.

1048. Petersen, Carol. JS (in German) (1975).

a) Warner, Ronald C. SQ, 10 (Summer-Fall 1977), 116-18.

1049. Pocock, Douglas C. D. (ed.). Humanistic Geography and Literature (1981).

a) Wilson, Jerry W. SQ, 15 (Winter-Spring 1982), 64-65.

1050. Prabhakar, S. S. JS: A Study ... (1976).

a) Govoni, Mark W. SQ, 14 (Summer-Fall 1981), 116-17.

1051. Pratt, John Clark. JS: A Critical Essay (1970).

a) Astro, Richard. SQ, 5 (Spring 1972), 47-49.

1052. Riggs, Susan F. (ed.). A Catalogue of the JS Collection at Stanford University (1980).

a) Moore, Thomas J. SQ, 15 (Winter-Spring 1982), 58-60.

1053. Sakamoto, Masayuki, and Iwao Iwamoto (eds.). Modern American Short Stories (1975).

a) Hirose, Hidekazu. SQ, 10 (Winter 1977), 21-22.

1054. Salzman, Jack, and Barry Wallenstein (eds.). Years of Protest (1967).

a) Grinnell, James W. SQ, 5 (Winter 1972), 22-23.

1055. Sano, Minoru (ed.). "The Gift" from The Red Pony (1974).

a) Yano, Shigeharu. SQ, 10 (Spring 1977), 57-58.

1056. Satyanarayana, M. R. JS: A Study in the Theme of Compassion (1977).

a) Smith, Juanita J. SQ, 13 (Summer-Fall 1980), 119-20.

1057. Schmitz, Anne-Marie. In Search of S (1978).

a) Noto, Sal. SQ, 13 (Winter-Spring 1980), 42-44.

1058. Shasky, Florian J., and Susan F. Riggs (eds.). Letters to Elizabeth: A Selection of Letters from JS to Elizabeth Otis (1978).

a) Hayman, Lee Richard. SQ, 13 (Summer-Fall 1980), 113-15.

1059. Simmonds, Roy S. S's Literary Achievement (SMS, No. 6), ed. T. Hayashi, 1976.

a) Spies, George H. III. SQ, 11 (Summer-Fall 1978), 117-19.

1060. Sinnott, Edmund W. The Biology of the Spirit (1975).

a) Peterson, Richard F. SQ, 7 (Winter 1974), 25-26.

1061. Sreenivasan, K. JS: A Study of His Novels (1980).

a) Tammaro, Thomas M. SQ, 14 (Summer-Fall 1981), 123-25.

1062. Steinbeck, John. The Acts of King Arthur and His Noble Knights, ed. Chase Horton (1976).

a) Black, Robert. Denver Quarterly, 114 (Winter 1977), 206-09.

b) Ditsky, John. AL, 49 (January 1978), 633-35.

c) Fuller, Edmund. Wall Street Journal, November 18, 1976. p. 22.

d) Gardener, John. New York Times Book Review, October 24, 1976. pp. 31-32, 34, 36.

e) McDaniel, Barbara. West Coast R, 576 (January 1978), 648.

f) McKenzie, Alice. Clearwater Sun (Florida), December 26, 1976. p. 6F.

g) Morsberger, Robert E. WAL, 12 (August 1977), 163-65.

h) Mosedale, John. Times (London), December 19, 1976. p. 1.

i) Moynihan, Michael. Sunday Times, January 2, 1976. p. 3.

j) Shippey, T. A. TLS, 536 (April 29, 1977), 617.

k) Simmonds, Roy S. SQ, 10 (Spring 1977), 52-57.

1063. _____. Burning Bright (1950; 1979).

a) Dunbar, Maurice. SQ, 13 (Winter-Spring 1980), 44-45.

1064. _____. Cannery Row (Film) (1982).

a) Andrews, Rena. Denver Post, February 13, 1982. D, 1.

b) Arnold, William. Seattle Post-Intelligencer, February 12, 1982. D, 26.

c) Baron, David. New Orleans Times, February 12, 1982. p. 4.

d) Barrett, Jim. Salinas Californian, July 7, 1980. 5 D.

e) Berman, Pat. The State and the Columbia (SC) Record, February 19, 1982. p. 3-D.

f) Blowen, Michael. Boston Globe, February 12, 1982. p. 36.

g) Butler, Robert W. Kansas City Star, February 14, 1982. p. 42A.

h) Calen, Herb. San Francisco Chronicle, January 8, 1982. p. 21.

i) Canby, Vincent. New York Times, February 12, 1982. p. 22; C 10.

j) Chase, Donald. Horizon, 24 (January-February 1982), pp. 52-57.

k) Crist, Judith. SR, 9 (March 1982), 55.

l) Davis, Charles. Monterey Peninsula Herald, January 29, 1982.

m) Ebert, Roger. Chicago Sun-Times, February 12, 1982. p. 41-42.

n) Eden, David. Minneapolis Star, February 12, 1982. p. 5C.

o) Frymer, Murry. San Jose Mercury, February 12, 1982. p. 7C.

p) Kessler, Pamela. Washington Post, February 12, 1982. p. 11.

q) Leyde, Tom. Salinas Californian, January 23, 1982. p. 26.

r) Reed, Rex. New York Daily News, February 10, 1982. p. 46.

s) Reich, Howard. Chicago Tribune, February 14, 1982. VI, 12-13; February 17, 1982, II, 9.

t) Scott, Vernon. Mainichi Daily News (Japan), June, 11, 1980. p. 9.

u) Stone, Judy. San Francisco Chronicle, February 11, 1982. p. 65; February 13, 1982. p. 34; February 14, 1982. pp. 20-21.

v) Thomas, Kevin. Los Angeles Times, February 12, 1982. VI, 1, 19.

w) Warga, Wayne. Los Angeles Times, February 8, 1981. p. 34.

1065. _____. East of Eden (Film) (1981).

a) Bradburg, Malcolm. New Statesman, 91 (March 12, 1976), 328-29.

b) O'Connor, John J. New York Times, February 6, 1981. C22.

c) Prendergast, Roy M. Film Music: A Neglected Art. New York: Norton, 1977. pp. 110-11.

d) Wilson, Jerry W. SQ, 14 (Summer-Fall 1981), 127-29.

1066. _____. The Grapes of Wrath (play) (1978).

a) Morsberger, Robert S. SQ, 11 (Summer-Fall 1978), 112-15.

1067. _____. Of Mice and Men (play).

a) Atkinson, Brooks. New Republic, 179 (January 25, 1979), 18.

b) Bernheimer, Martin. Los Angeles Times, March 18, 1974. VI, 1.

c) Christon, Lawrence. Los Angeles Times, February 11, 1977. IV, 26.

d) Clurman, Harold. Nation, 220 (January 19, 1975), 27.

e) Ditsky, John. SQ, 8 (Summer-Fall 1975), 107-09.

f) _____. SQ, 14 (Summer-Fall 1981), 130-31.

g) Forscey, Suzon. Los Angeles Herald-Examiner, November 17, 1973. B, 6.

h) Gil, Brendon. New Yorker, 50 (December 30, 1974), 52.

i) Glorer, William. Los Angeles Times, December 24, 1974. II, 13.

j) Gottfried, Martin. SR, 6 (January 20, 1979), 57.

k) Guinn, John. Detroit Free Press, September 28, 1980. 3D.

l) Hoover, Marjorie L. New Republic, 172 (January 25, 1975), 18.

m) Hughes, Catherine. America, 132 (January 18, 1975), 36.

n) Kamerman, L. Calgary Herald, November 16, 1979. [n. p.].

o) Kanfer, Stefan. Time, 104 (December 30, 1974), 53.

p) Kauffmann, Stanley. New Republic, 172 (January 25, 1975), 18.

q) Mahoney, John C. Los Angeles Times, October 6, 1976. IV, 12.

r) Morsberger, Robert E. , and Katherine M. Ma-

gill's Survey of the Cinema. Englewood Cliffs,
N. J.: Salem Press, 1980 [n. p.].

s) Sanders, Vicki. Berkshire Eagle, May 1, 1976.
[n. p.].

t) Schwartz, Sol. Akron Beacon Journal, October
28, 1975. p. 12.

u) Spencer, Brad. Cross and Cresent, [n. v.] (May
1974), 15-16.

1068. _____. A Russian Journal (1948; 1978).

a) Simpson, Arthur L., Jr. SQ, 5 (Spring 1972),
53-54.

1069. _____. Sea of Cortez (1941; 1971).

a) Hozeski, Bruce W., and Richard Astro. SQ, 6
(Spring 1973), 57-58.

1070. _____. Steinbeck: A Life in Letters, eds. Elaine
Steinbeck and Robert Wallsten (1975).

a) Allen, Walter. TLS, May 14, 1976. [n. p.].

b) Bradbury, Malcolm. New Statesman, 91 (March
12, 1976), 328-29.

c) Chambers, C. A. Virginia QR, 52 (Summer
1976), 527.

d) Cohen, George. Chicago Tribune, October 19,
1975. VII, 11-13.

e) Ditsky, John. Southern Humanities R, 12 (Winter
1978), 74-76.

f) Dollen, Charles. Best Sellers, 35 (February
1976), 358.

g) French, Warren. AL, 48 (November 1976), 408.

h) Green, Benny. Spectator, March 13, 1976. p.
22.

i) Holloway, David. Daily Telegraph, March 18,
1976. p. 13.

j) King, Francis. Sunday Telegraph, March 14,
1976. p. 16.

k) Levathes, Kiki. New York Daily News, July 28, 1974. [n. p.].

l) Levin, Bernard. Observer, March 28, 1976. p. 31.

m) Lewis, R. W. B. SR, 3 (October 18, 1975), 11.

n) McDaniel, Barbara A. West Coast R, 55 (January 1978), 648.

o) Maloff, Saul. New York Times Book R, October 26, 1975. p. 5.

p) Marvin, J. R. Library Journal, 100 (September 15, 1975), 1624.

q) Morsberger, Robert E. WAL, 11 (August 1976), 183-85.

r) Spies, George H. , III. SQ, 9 (Spring 1976), 55-57.

s) Starr, Kevin. New Republic, 173 (November 22, 1975), 25.

t) Theroux, Paul. Times (London), March 8, 1976. p. 7.

u) Watt, F. W. Queen's Q, 123 (Spring 1978), 529.

1071. _____. Viva Zapata!, ed. Robert Morsberger (1975).

   a) Spies, George H. , III. SQ, 9 (Winter 1976), 29-30.

1072. Stuckey, W. J. (ed.). The Pulitzer Prize Novels (1966).

   a) Gadziola, David. SQ, 6 (Summer 1973), 84-87.

1073. Tedlock, E. W. , Jr. , and C. V. Wicker (eds.). Steinbeck and His Critics (1957; 1969).

   a) Gadziola, David. SQ, 5 (Summer-Fall 1972), 115-16.

1074. Valjean, Nelson. JS: The Errant Knight (1975).

   a) DeMott, Robert. SJS, 1 (November 1975), 136-39.

b) Freeman, J. L. Best Sellers, 35 (July 1975), 108.

c) McWilliams, Carey. Nation, 221 (August 30, 1975), 154.

d) Spies, George H., III. SQ, 9 (Spring 1976), 57-58.

e) Willingham, J. R. Library Journal, 100 (July 1975), 134.

1075. Walcutt, Charles Child. Man's Changing Mask: Modes and Methods of Characterization in Fiction (1969).

a) Hakutani, Yoshinobu. SQ, 13 (Summer-Fall 1980), 110-13.

1076. Watanabe, Masao (ed.). The Scientific Thought in American Literature (1974) (in Japanese).

a) Sugiyama, Takahiko. SQ, 10 (Summer-Fall 1977), 120-22.

1077. Watkins, Floyd C. In Time and Place: Some Origins of American Fiction (1977).

a) Moore, Thomas J. SQ, 13 (Winter-Spring 1980), 47-49.

1078. Watt, F. W. S (1962; 1978).

a) Moore, Thomas J. SQ, 13 (Winter-Spring 1980), 49-51.

b) Spies, George H., III. SQ, 5 (Spring 1972), 55-56.

1079. Weber, Tom. All the Hewes Are Dead: The Ecology of S's Cannery Row (1971).

a) Mammola, Joseph L. SQ, 8 (Summer-Fall 1975), 112-14.

1080. Yano, Shigeharu. The Current of S's World (1978).

a) Hirose, Hidekazu. SQ, 13 (Winter-Spring 1980), 45-46.

APPENDIX 1: A SELECTED LIST OF STANDARD REFERENCE GUIDES CONSULTED

Abstracts of English Studies

American Humanities Index

American Literary Scholarship/An Annual

Annual Bibliography of English Language & Literature, ed.
Marjory Rigby, et al.

Annual bibliography published in such journals as:

American Literature;

Journal of Modern Literature;

Modern Drama;

Modern Fiction Studies;

Twentieth Century Literature; etc.

Bibliographic Index

Biography Index

Book Review Digest

Book Review Index

British Humanities Index

Cumulative Book Index

Dissertation Abstracts International

Education Index

Essays and General Literature Index

Humanities Index

Index to Book Reviews in the Humanities

MLA Bibliography

Readers' Guide to Periodical Literature

Steinbeck bibliographies: See "Bibliographies" (283-331).

Subject Guide to Books in Print

N. B. : To identify each journal or newspaper, etc. , consult Ulrich's International Periodicals Directory or Ayer's Directory of Newspapers and Periodicals or Standard Periodicals Directory.

Agora (State University of New York College at Potsdam)
Agricultural History
Air California Magazine
Akron Beacon Journal
America
American Examiner
American Literature
American Quarterly
American Studies
American Studies in Scandinavia (Norway)
American Transcendental Quarterly
Antioch Review
Argosy
Asphodel (Doshisha Women's College, Japan)
Atlantic
Australian Literary Studies (Australia)
Avon

Berkshire Eagle (Pittsfield, Me.)
Best Sellers
Book-of-the-Month-Club News
Books and Arts
Books and Bookmen
Boston Globe
Brief
Bulletin of Ibaraki Christian Junior College (Japan)
Bulletin of Reitaku University (Japan)

Calgary Herald (Calgary, Alberta, Canada)
CEA Critic
Chicago Sun Times
Chicago Tribune
Christian Science Monitor
Chu-shikoku Studies in American Literature (Japan)

Cimarron Review (Oklahoma
State University)
CLA Journal
Clearwater Sun (Florida)
Coast Magazine
Collector
College English
Collier's
Colorado Quarterly
Contemporary Communication
(London)
Coronet
Cresset
Criticism
Cross and Crescent
CTA Journal

Daily Express
Daily Mail
Daily Sketch
Daily Telegraph
Daily Union Democrat (Sonora,
Cal.)
Dalhousie Review
Denver Post
Denver Quarterly
Detroit Free Press
Discourse

English Journal
English Review
Esquire
Evening Standard (England)
Explicator

Fairpress (Westport, Conn.)
Ford Times
Forum (Houston, Texas)

Genre
Good Housekeeping

Harper's
Harper's Bazaar
Hartford Studies in Litera-
ture
Harvard Library Bulletin
Holiday
Horizon
Hosei University General
Education Quarterly
(Japan)
Hungarian Quarterly (Buda-
pest)

The Imprint of the Stanford
Libraries Associates
Indian Journal of American
Studies (India)
Indian Journal of English
Studies (India)
Indian Studies in American
Fiction (India)
Interpretations: Studies in
Language and Literature

Journal of American Studies
Journal of Ethnic Studies
Journal of Modern Litera-
ture
Journal of Narrative Tech-
nique
Journal of Obirin Univer-
sity and Junior College
(Japan)
Journal of the Faculty of
Liberal Arts (Yamagu-
chi University, Japan)
Journal of the School of
Language (India)

Kagoshima Studies in Eng-
lish Language and Liter-
ature (Japan)
Kansai University Essays
and Studies (Japan)

Kansai University Literary
Quarterly (Japan)
Kansas City Star
Kansas English
Kaohsiung Teachers College
Journal (Taiwan)
Kemmei Women's Junior Col-
lege Bulletin (Japan)
Knight
Kumazawa University Foreign
Language Bulletin (Japan)
Kure Technical College Report
(Japan)
Kurume University Journal
(Japan)
Kwartalinik Neofilologizny
(Poland)
Kyushu American Literature
(Japan)

Ladies Home Journal
Lethebridge Herald (Canada)
Library Chronicle (University
of Texas)
Library Journal
Life
Lilliput
Literature and Ideology (Canada)
Literature/Film Quarterly
Los Angeles Herald-Examiner
Los Angeles Times

McCall's
Mainichi Daily News (Japan)
Manchester Guardian (England)
Markham Review (Wagner Col-
lege, N. Y.)
Massachusetts Review
Mercury (San Jose, Cal.)
Michigan Quarterly Review
Minneapolis Star
Modern Drama
Modern Fiction Studies
Monterey Beacon
Monterey Peninsula Herald
(Cal.)

Nation
National Observer
NEA Journal
Negro History Bulletin
NEMLA Newsletter
Die Neueren Sprachen
(Germany)
New Blackfriars (Univer-
sity of Leeds, England)
New Hungarian Quarterly
New Orleans Times
New Republic
New Statesman
New York Daily News
New York Folklore Quar-
terly
New York Herald Tribune
New York Times
New Yorker
News Chronicle
Newsday
Newsweek
Nippon University Litera-
ture and Science Re-
search Report (Japan)
North American Review
North Dakota Quarterly
Notes on Modern American
Literature

Observer
Occident
Osmania Journal of English
Studies (India)

Pacific Historian
Pacific Weekly
Palo Alto Times (Cal.)
Papers on Language and
Literature
Paris Review (Flushing,
N. Y.)
Persica (Okayama Univer-
sity, Japan)
Philadelphia Bulletin
Phoenix (Japan)

Photography
PMLA
Popular Science
Portland Oregonian
Progressive Weekly
Punch

Quarterly Newsletter (Book
  Club of California)
Queen's Quarterly

RE: Artes Liberales (Austin
  State University, Texas)
Reader's Digest
Reitaku University Quarterly
  (Japan)
Research Report of Yatsushiro
  National College of Tech-
  nology (Japan)
Research Studies
Religion in Life

Salinas Californian
San Francisco Chronicle
San Francisco Examiner
San Francisco News
San Jose Mercury
San Jose Studies
Saturday Review
Scene
Scholastic
School Library Journal
Science Digest
Seattle Post-Intelligence
Series in English Language and
  Literature (India)
Serif (Kent State University
  Library, Kent, Ohio)
Shimane University Law and
  Letters College Quarterly
  (Japan)
South Dakota Review
Southern Humanities Review
Southern Review

Southwest Review
Southwestern American
  Literature
Spartan Daily (San Jose
  State University, Cal.)
Spectator
Stage
Stanford Magazine
Stanford Spectator
The State and the Columbia
  (S. C.) Record
Steinbeck Collector
Steinbeck Monograph Series
Steinbeck Quarterly
Story
Strand Magazine
Studies in English Litera-
  ture (Japan)
Studies in Short Fiction
Sun Magazine (Philadelphia,
  Pa.)
Sunday Citizen
Sunday Times (London)
Sunset (Menlo Park, Cal.)

Thought
Time
Times (London)
Times Literary Supplement
  (London)
True
Twentieth Century Litera-
  ture

University of Kansas City
  Review
University of Windsor Re-
  view (Canada)

Virginia Quarterly Review
Vogue

Wall Street Journal

Washington Post
Weekend Telegraph (England)
West Coast Review
Western American Literature
Western Review
Wings
Writer's Yearbook

INDEX
(Numbers refer to entries, not pages unless preceded by
"p." or "pp.")

123

Amex, Cathy (Of Mice and Men) 585
Anderson, Arthur Cummings 454
Anderson, Sherwood 489, 873, 943
Andrews, Rena 1004(a)
ANIMAL SYMBOLISM/IMAGERY 456, 680, 851, 921
Argosy (British) 326
Armo, Peter 50
Arnold, William 1064(b)
ARTHURIAN THEME 428, 633, 665, 713, 738-739, 895, 901
ARTICLES/ESSAYS IN JOURNALS, MAGAZINES, AND BOOKS
  490-975
ARTIST AS MAGICIAN 639
Asano, Toshio 492
"Aspects of Steinbeck's Thought and Writing" (Conference)
  437
Astro, Richard 332-334, 344, 357, 360, 371, 382, 383, 411-
  412, 435-436, 440, 493-503, 505-506, 518, 561, 584,
  589, 598, 707, 763, 786, 796, 812, 889, 917, 926, 946,
  978-981, 992(a), 1030(d), 1051(a), 1069(a)
Atkinson, Brooks 1967(a)
Atkinson, David W. 1028(b)
Atticus 213
AUTOMOBILE 911
Autrey, Max L. 507

Bach, Bert C. 23
Barbour, Brian M. 508, 980(a), 1014(a)
Barnaby Rudge (Dickens) 913
Barnes, Douglas R. 56
Baron, David 1964(c)
Barrett, Jim 1064(d)
Beach, Joseph Warren 982 (a)
Beatty, Sandra 509-510
Bedford, Richard C. 511-513
Bellman, Samuel I. 514
Bemelmans, L. 182
Benardete, Jane 515
Benchley, Nathaniel 149(a), 334(a)
Bennett, George 22
Bennett, Robert 413
Benson, Deborah 490
Benson, Frederick R. 335
Benson, Jackson J. 336, 516-520, 1006(a-b)
Bentley, Nicholas 234
Benton, Robert M. 521-525, 979(a)
Berman, Pat 1064(e)

Grover, Katharine 250, 256a
Grover, Sherwood 250
Guerin, Wilfred 683
Guggenheim, Patterson ("Alicia") 257
Guinn, John 1067(k)
Gunn, Drewey Wayne 683(a)
Gurko, Leo 684

"Hadleyburg" (Twain) 743
Hagopian, John V. 44
Hagy, Boyd Frederick 466
Hakutani, Yoshinobu 648, 1008, 1075(a)
Hamaguchi, Osamu 685, 686, 1011(a), 1121(b), 1045(a)
Hamalian, Leo 42
Hamby, James A. 687-688, 977(a)
Hammerstein, Oscar 73
Hammond, Frank L. 226
Hancock, Joan 56
Hargrave, John 689
Harmon, Robert B. 298-299, 451, 1009, 1010
Harrity, Richard 128
Hart, Harvey 1065(d)
Hart, James D. 256a
Hashiguchi, Yasuo 430, 443, 690, 1011, 1023
　"Report of the Annual Meetings of the Steinbeck Society of
　　Japan (1978-　)" see SQ, 11 (Summer-Fall 1978), 124-
　　25; SQ, 13 (Winter-Spring 1980), 63; SQ, 14 (Winter-
　　Spring 1981), 57-58
Hawley, Ethan Allen (The Winter) 938
Hayashi, Tetsumaro 284, 300-307, 308-313, 317-318,
　　321, 329, 344, 357, 367(a), 369-374, 388-393, 423,
　　426-427, 430-433, 435-436, 438, 442-443, 452, 493,
　　495, 499-500, 505-506, 509, 521, 523, 525, 553-554,
　　563-564, 571, 576-578, 584, 589-590, 595, 597-598,
　　607-608, 611, 618, 621, 632-633, 639, 644-645, 647,
　　652, 664, 666-667, 670-671, 675, 679, 691-704, 709,
　　712, 728, 739, 763, 767-769, 783, 785, 788, 795-796,
　　798, 800, 809-814, 821, 838, 841-843, 844, 847-849,
　　850, 853, 886, 889, 895, 897, 899, 900-903, 907, 910,
　　913, 917, 920, 923, 924, 935, 951, 966, 979(c), 980,
　　1007(b), 1012-1025, 1033(a)
Hayman, Lee Richard 297, 313, 705-706, 1007, 1029(a),
　　1058(a)
Hedgpeth, Joel W. 344-346, 371, 394, 412, 440, 494, 516,
　　518, 707-709, 786, 926, 946, 981, 1026